THE
ATOMIC BOMB
ON MY BACK

THE
ATOMIC BOMB
ON MY BACK

Verbatim Account of Taniguchi Sumiteru

Compiled by
Hisashi Tomokuni

Published by
Rootstock Publishing

First Printing: August 9, 2020

The Atomic Bomb On My Back
Copyright © 2020 Japan Confederation of A-and H-Bomb Sufferers Organizations

All Rights Reserved.

Release Date: August 9, 2020
Softcover ISBN: 978-1-57869-040-4
eBook: 978-1-57869-041-1
LCCN: 2020909026

Rootstock Publishing

Published by Rootstock Publishing
an imprint of Multicultural Media, Inc.,
27 Main Street, Suite 6
Montpelier, VT 05602 USA
www.rootstockpublishing.com
info@rootstockpublishing.com

The original Japanese book "Genbaku wo seotte (Having A-bomb on My Back)" was published in August 2014 by Nishinippon Shimbunsha

No part of this book may be reproduced, stored in a retrieval system, or transmitted in any form or by any means, electronic, mechanical, photo- copying, recording, or otherwise, without the prior written permission of the author, except as provided by USA copyright law.

Interior design by Eddie Vincent (ed.vincent@encirclepub.com)
Cover design by Deirdre Wait/Enc Graphic Services
Printed in the USA

CONTENTS

Introduction to English Version by Peter Kuznick xv
Preface: *As Long As My Life Continues* by Taniguchi Sumiteru 1
Foreword: *My Wish for This Story to Be Read by as Many People as Possible* by Hiroshi Taka 3

Chapter 1: Struck by the Atomic Bomb:
The Beginning of My Endless Agony 7

   Scars on my back still aching 7
   Mother's death shapes my life 9
   Nagasaki, a city of military factories 11
   Draft papers delivered at midnight 13
   August 9, the fateful day 14
   Escaping from hell 16
   Guarding the mails to the end 19
   Bleeding starts on the 6th day 22

Chapter 2: Life in Hospital for 3 Years and 7 Months 23

   A can full of raw cow livers 23
   Transfer to the Omura Naval Hospital 25
   "Kill me!" 26
   Filmed by U.S. investigation team 28
   My medical record 30
   The bold doctor and I 32
   Increasing anxiety before leaving the hospital 33

Chapter 3: Adolescent Years That I Declared to Live 36

   Tearful reunion with my grandmother 36
   An anxious day - I returned to work 38
   Anger towards ABCC 40
   Heartbreak and attempted suicide 41
   Fighting against discrimination 43
   I finally take off my shirt 44

Chapter 4: Fear of Nuclear Weapons Enters the Spotlight 47

The Lucky Dragon No.5 is exposed to H-bomb fallout *47*
From Suginami, the movement spread nationwide. *49*
The World Conference against A and H Bombs *51*
"Marriage" of the Youth and Maidens. *53*
Founding of the Nagasaki Council of A-Bomb Survivors
(Nagasaki Hisaikyo) *55*
Hibakusha begin to speak out. *57*
Message to the world *59*
Hibakusha movement bears fruit *62*
Hibakusha's situation not understood *64*
Trip to East Germany for medical treatment *66*

Chapter 5: My Life Partner 69

First meeting with Eiko. *70*
My anxiety during the honeymoon *72*
Joy of becoming a father *74*
Supported by family *76*
A decision to visit a beach *78*
Living with my wife for half a century . . . .

Chapter 6: In the Midst of the Storm Splitting the Movement 80

Japan shaken by the Japan-U.S. Security Treaty *80*
A crack in the anti-A and H bomb movement *82*
In a storm of the movement's split
Hidankyo becomes dysfunctional *84*
Hibakusha and Vietnam *86*
Aiming to unite the movement *88*

Chapter 7: "Reddened Back" Shown to the Public 93

My reddened back shown to the public. *93*
Pushed onto center stage *95*
"Pledge for peace". *97*
Nuclear-powered ship, 'Mutsu'. *99*
Continuing protests against nuclear tests. *101*

Chapter 8: Appealing to the World to Face the Reality
of the A-Bombing 104

Attending international conference *104*
Reactions from abroad *106*
Give us back our humanity *109*
A sense of exaltation I had never felt *110*

    Postman of Nagasaki *113*
    Appearing on a French TV show *114*
    A reunion after a half century. *116*
    Looking for colleagues' remains. *117*

Chapter 9: Calling for the Expansion of
Hibakusha Relief Measures 120

    For expansion of relief measures for the hibakusha. *120*
    Summoned as a witness by the Diet *122*
    Anger over the "endurance theory". *125*
    Our demand for State compensation *126*
    Lawsuits for official recognition on A-Bomb diseases *128*
    Achievement of the collective lawsuits *130*

Chapter 10: Road to the Abolition of Nuclear Weapons............. 134

    Logic of the massive nuclear country: U.S.A. *134*
    Disseminating the facts through civilian exchanges. *136*
    Stomped wreath. *138*
    Advisory opinion of the International Court of Justice *140*
    Still a long way to go toward eliminating nuclear weapons. .. *142*
    Nominated for the Nobel Peace Prize *144*
    Arrival of President Obama *146*
    Appeal at the NPT Review Conference. *148*
    Has the world changed yet? *149*

Chapter 11: Before We Hand over Our Work to Descendants 152

    Death of Sen-chan *152*
    Failure in health, anxiety and my last word. *154*
    Accident at Fukushima Daiichi Nuclear Power Plant *155*
    Meeting with Truman's grandson. *157*
    Inspired by encounters *159*
    For the love of my hometown. *160*
    Let Nagasaki be the last A-bombed site *163*

Chronological Record of the Life of Taniguchi Sumiteru 166

Afterword by Hisashi Tomokuni. 171

Note: This book is a compilation of verbatim accounts of Taniguchi Sumiteru: "Having the A-Bomb on My Back" published in Nishi-Nippon Shimbun from July 8 to October 9, 2013, with some additions and alterations. Ages and titles of the characters are as of the date of the original publication.

The Atomic Bomb On My Back

Upholding the photo of his "Reddened Back", Sumiteru appeals for a nuclear weapon-free world at the 2010 NPT Review Conference

Taniguchi Sumiteru

At the graduation of Higher Course of Fuchi Primary School

Sumiteru, age 13, at home on a summer day

Sumiteru enters a primary school — with Grandmother Taga and Grandfather Sakutaro

The Atomic Bomb On My Back

With close friends at the telegraph office (Sumiteru in front)

With his colleague's encouragement, Sumiteru took off his shirt and had a dip in the sea

Taniguchi Sumiteru

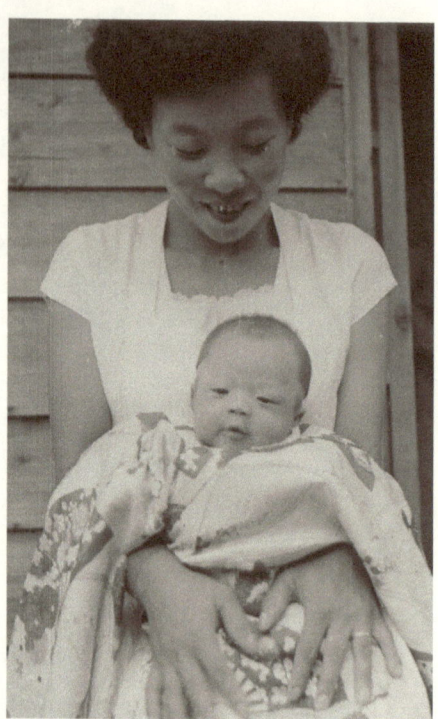

Eiko with the newly-born daughter Sumie

Sumiteru with his wife Eiko, daughter Sumie and son Hideo in front of his house

The Atomic Bomb On My Back

At the 25th anniversary of the Nagasaki A-bomb Youth and Maidens Association
(Sumiteru sits in the front row, 4th from right)

Sumiteru joins the Peace March in Greece (1985)

Sumiteru stands in front of Suginami Public Hall, one of the workshop venues of the Third World Conference against A and H Bombs (1957)

Taniguchi Sumiteru

"I wish you all the best in your work for the abolition of nuclear weapons," Sumiteru tells UN Secretary General Ban Ki-moon as they shake hands (2010).

Sumiteru and Eiko near their house overlooking Nagasaki Port

INTRODUCTION TO ENGLISH VERSION

Prof. Peter Kuznick, Professor of History and Director of the Nuclear Studies Institute at American University

TANIGUCHI SUMITERU WAS ONE OF the "lucky" ones. He lived a long and productive life. He married and fathered two healthy children who gave him four grandchildren and two great grandchildren. He had a long career in Japan's postal and telegraph services. As a leader in Japan's anti-nuclear movement, he addressed thousands of audiences and hundreds of thousands of people. He traveled to at least 23 countries. The organizations in which he played a prominent role were nominated several times for the Nobel Peace Prize.

Many of the more than 250,000 who lived in Nagasaki on August 9, 1945 were not so lucky. Tens of thousands were killed instantly by the plutonium core atomic bomb the U.S. dropped that day from the B29 Bockscar, captained by Major Charles Sweeney. The bomb, nicknamed "Fat Man," exploded with a force equivalent to 21 kilotons of TNT and wiped out an area that covered three square miles, shattering windows eleven miles away. Some 74,000 were dead by the end of the year. The death toll reached 140,000 by 1950. Included among the victims were thousands of Korean slave laborers, who toiled in Japanese mines, fields, and factories. Since then, atomic bomb-related injuries and illnesses have claimed thousands more victims and caused immense suffering to many of the survivors.

The scene of death and destruction defied description. Corpses, many of which had been charred by the blast, lay everywhere. Susan Southard, in her groundbreaking book *Nagasaki: Life After Nuclear War*, describes the scene that U.S. occupation troops encountered when they landed on September 23, 1945: "The Urakami Valley had vanished from existence, corpses were burning on cremation pyres, skulls and bones were piled on the ground, and people were walking through the ruins with beleaguered and empty expressions." Among the troops was Keith Lynch, a sailor from Nebraska. Lynch wrote to his parents that he had just seen "a sight I hope my children, if I am so fortunate, will never have to see, hear of, or ever think of. It was horrible and when you get to thinking, unbelievable.... Such a thing as I saw yesterday cannot be described in words. You have to see it and I hope no one ever has to see such a thing again."

The death toll was even higher and the destruction greater in Hiroshima, which the U.S. had obliterated three days earlier with a uranium core atomic bomb. There, some 200,000 were dead by 1950. The Nagasaki bomb was more powerful than the one that leveled Hiroshima, but damage was limited by the fact that the bomb missed its target and that the mountains surrounding Nagasaki, which is located in a valley, contained the blast. However, in Urakami Valley, where the bomb landed, nearly 70 percent of the population perished.

Questions about the atomic bombings have persisted ever since those fateful days in August 1945. Renowned journalist Edward R. Murrow asked President Truman in a 1958 television interview, "When the bomb was dropped, the war was near to ending anyway. Was this the result of a miscalculation of the Japanese potential? Was our intelligence faulty in this area?" Truman correctly denied that he had miscalculated or that the intelligence had been faulty. He knew exactly what he was doing. For months, in fact, Allied intelligence had been accurately reporting Japan's growing desire to quit and the fact that there were alternatives to using atomic bombs to end the war. On July 6, 1945, in preparation for the Potsdam Conference, the Combined Intelligence Committee of the Combined Chiefs of Staff issued a top secret "Estimate of the Enemy Situation." The section on the "Possibility of Surrender" clearly stated:

> *The Japanese ruling groups are aware of the desperate military situation and are increasingly desirous of a compromise peace, but still find unconditional surrender unacceptable... .a considerable portion of the Japanese population now consider absolute military defeat to be probable....An entry of the Soviet Union into the war would finally convince the Japanese of the inevitability of complete defeat.*

Truman recognized the growing desperation of Japanese leaders, whose citizens were becoming increasingly demoralized. The U.S. had firebombed and largely destroyed more than 100 Japanese cities, leaving millions homeless. With the food supply shrinking and the transportation system in tatters, starvation loomed. Energy supplies had run so low that new Japanese pilots could barely undertake the training flights needed to prepare for battle. U.S. forces had decimated Japan's air force and navy. And, as the July 6 report indicated, Japanese leaders were looking for a way out and American leaders knew it. Truman described the intercepted July 18 cable between officials in Tokyo and Moscow as "the telegram from the Jap emperor asking for peace." Based on other recently intercepted cables, his close advisors concurred. They knew that giving the Japanese assurances that they could keep the emperor would likely bring surrender. Secretary of War Henry Stimson pushed Truman and Secretary of State James Byrnes to drop the demand for unconditional surrender and inform the Japanese that the emperor could stay. Most of Truman's top military and civilian advisors joined Stimson in that endeavor. General Douglas MacArthur, Southwest Pacific Supreme Commander, later declared, somewhat overoptimistically, that the Japanese would have happily surrendered in May if U.S. leaders had changed the surrender terms.

But that was not the only way to induce surrender without use of the atomic bombs. U.S. leaders could also have waited for the Soviets to declare war against Japan and begin the invasion of Japanese-occupied territories and perhaps Japan itself. Truman was confident that this would do the trick. When he got Stalin's confirmation at Potsdam that the Soviets were coming in, he wrote in his diary on July 17, "He'll be in the Jap War on August 15. Fini Japs when that comes about." He wrote to his wife the next day, exulting, "We'll end the war a year sooner now, and think of the kids who won't be killed!"

But Truman's crime goes beyond slaughtering innocent civilians. Making Truman's actions totally indefensible was the fact that Truman knew that he was beginning a process that could end all life on the planet and said so on at least three occasions. While at Potsdam, most famously, he reacted to an in-depth briefing on the incredible power of the Alamogordo bomb test by shuddering, "It may be the fire destruction prophesied in the Euphrates Valley Era, after Noah and his fabulous Ark." Many scientists knew he wasn't exaggerating. Physicist Edward Teller had been pushing for immediate development of hydrogen bombs for years. Fellow Hungarian Leo Szilard warned that the destructive force in such bombs could be almost unlimited in size. Los Alamos scientific director J. Robert Oppenheimer had earlier warned top government and military leaders that within three years the U.S. would likely have weapons between 700 and 7,000 times as powerful as the relatively primitive bomb that would flatten Hiroshima. In less than a decade, scientists were indeed testifying before Congress about the feasibility of developing a thermonuclear explosive with the power of 700,000 Hiroshima bombs. Insanity was the order of the day. As Lewis Mumford wrote, "madmen," calmly, rationally planning annihilation, had seized the levers of power. As Taniguchi Sumiteru understood, they have not relinquished it since.

The question that plagues many historians is not whether the bombs needed to be used to prevent an invasion that was not even scheduled to begin for another three months against a foe that had clearly been defeated. Obviously, they did not. Seven of America's eight five star officers in 1945 are on record saying as much. Admiral William D. Leahy, Truman's personal Chief of Staff, said that in using the atomic bombs, the U.S. "adopted an ethical standard common to the barbarians of the dark ages." Even the National Museum of the U.S. Navy in Washington, DC acknowledges that the vast death and destruction wreaked by atomic bombings "made little impact on the Japanese military. However, the Soviet invasion of Manchuria…changed their minds." The question is not whether the atomic bombs were militarily or morally justifiable—they clearly were not. The question is why Truman chose to use them when he knew the end of the war was imminent and said so repeatedly and knew they were putting humanity on a glide path to annihilation.

As historians have increasingly come to realize, Truman had been obsessed with the Soviet Union since April 13, 1945—his first full day in office. His close advisors, most of whom had little if any influence upon Roosevelt, pushed him to act firmly to challenge Soviet actions in Europe. Truman's confrontation with Foreign Minister Molotov on April 23, in which he erroneously accused the Soviets of having broken their Yalta promises, marked how dramatically the wartime alliance between the U.S. and the U.S.S.R. had deteriorated in the 11 days since Roosevelt's death. James Byrnes, who became Truman's Secretary of State in early July but had been his most trusted advisor since his first day in office, and Gen. Leslie Groves, the driving force behind the Manhattan Project, both asserted that the Soviet Union loomed as the real target behind the bomb project. Byrnes told three visiting scientists in late May that the bomb was needed to reverse Soviet gains in Eastern Europe. Groves appalled physicist Joseph Rotblat, the future Nobel laureate who quit the project a few months later, when he said in March 1944, "You realize of course that the main purpose of this project is to subdue the Russians." Groves stated on another occasion, "There was never from about two weeks from the time I took charge of the Project any illusion on my part that Russia was our enemy, and the Project was conducted on that basis."

Taniguchi Sumiteru concurred with that assessment. In this moving memoir, he writes, "Some studies point out that the U.S. wanted to test the uranium and plutonium-type bombs to show off their military muscle and take the advantage in the post-World War II diplomacy. I agree with this perspective."

He understood fully and says directly that "nuclear weapons are weapons of annihilation." When he died in August 2017, 72 years after the atomic bombings, his anger had not abated. Those who work closely with Hibakusha (atomic bomb-affected persons) have often heard them say that they don't condemn U.S. leaders; they condemn war. In Kurosawa Akira's moving 1991 film *Rhapsody in August*, when the 80-year old grandmother Kane, whose husband had been killed in the Nagasaki bombing, learns of her four grandchildren's concern about her suffering at U.S. hands, she explains, "it was a long time ago that I felt bitter about America. It's been 45 years since grandpa died. Now I neither like nor dislike America. It was because of the war. The war was to blame." This sentiment was especially pervasive in Nagasaki where the response to the bombings was deliberately depoliticized by a form of Christian apologetics.

Visitors to Nagasaki quickly discover that the bomb missed its intended downtown target near the Mitsubishi shipbuilding and munitions manufacturing headquarters by two miles. It exploded instead above the Urakami Cathedral, East Asia's largest, in the center of the biggest Catholic community in Japan. Nagasaki's Catholic community dates back to the 16th century, but, after flourishing briefly, its members were persecuted and driven underground. The community didn't reemerge until the Meiji government lifted the ban against Christianity in 1873. There were approximately 14,000 Catholics in Urakami at the time of the atomic bombing. The one who did the most to shape the city's postwar narrative was Catholic doctor Nagai Takashi.

Nagai converted to Catholicism in 1934 after a one-year stint as a Japanese imperial army surgeon in Manchuria. During his second military tour from 1937 to 1940, he served in Nanjing at the time Japanese troops were carrying out the brutal massacre, commonly known as the "Rape of Nanjing." Upon his return to Japan, Nagai was decorated with the Order of the Rising Sun for his "bravery." Back in Japan, he served as Dean of the Department of Radiology at Nagasaki Medical University where he was diagnosed with leukemia in June 1945. He suffered another major blow two months later when his wife was killed in the atomic bombing, leaving him to raise his two young children.

Nagai worked tirelessly and heroically to help the victims of the bombing at a time when doctors and medical facilities were in desperately short supply. But, as Miyamoto Yuki has explained, it was his Biblical interpretation of the bombing that proved his most enduring, and controversial, legacy. This was best captured in a lecture he gave during a mass on November 23, 1945 in which he stated, "It was the providence of God that carried the bomb to that destination…Was Nagasaki, the only holy place in all Japan, not chosen as a victim, a pure lamb, to be slaughtered and burned on the altar of sacrifice to expiate the sins committed by humanity in the Second World War? Only when Nagasaki was burned did God accept the sacrifice. Hearing the cry of the human family. He inspired the emperor to issue the sacred decree by which the war was brought to an end." Nagai called upon Nagasaki's Catholics to "give thanks that Nagasaki had been chosen for the sacrifice."

Living in a tiny 43 square foot hut with his two young children, the charismatic Nagai, his health rapidly deteriorating, wrote fifteen books before his death in 1951. His classic work, *The Bells of Nagasaki*, was published in 1949 with the blessing of the occupation authorities and turned into a popular movie. Publication had been delayed for more than two years due to the strict censorship U.S. authorities imposed on discussions of the atomic bombs. GHQ, the General Headquarters of the Allied Powers, insisted he change the title from his original choice *The Curtain Rises on the Atomic Age*. With its new title, the book quickly became a bestseller and helped popularize the idea that the bombing was "God's Providence" and the Nagasaki Catholics were deliberately chosen for this "redemptive sacrifice."

In other writings, Nagai shifted the blame for the atomic bombing from the Americans to the Japanese themselves: "it is not the atomic bomb that gouged this huge hole in the Urakami basin. We dug it ourselves to the rhythm of military marches.... We turned the beautiful city of Nagasaki into a heap of ashes.... It is we the people who busily made warships and torpedoes."

As Otsuki Tomoe has shown in her dissertation and articles, Nagai's message of "forgiveness" and "reconciliation" was one that U.S. occupation authorities were more than happy to propagate. Gen. Douglas MacArthur, the Supreme Commander of the Allied Powers, had sought to replace Shinto influence in Japan with Christianity. Shinto, he believed, abetted militarism, while Christianity undergirded democracy. "Democracy and Christianity have much in common," he averred, "as practice of the former is impossible without giving faithful service to the fundamental concepts underlying the latter." Under MacArthur's command, GHQ officials worked hard to assist Nagasaki's Catholics during the postwar reconstruction of the city, paving the way for the city's new identity—an identity that Nagasaki governor Sugiyama Sojiro happily embraced two years after the bombing when he declared, "Nagasaki is the land of Christian martyrdom." As a result, the saying caught on that "Ikari no Hiroshima, inori no Nagasaki"—"Hiroshima rages, Nagasaki prays."

Taniguchi was part of a different Nagasaki. He raged rather

than prayed. When I met him in 1998, the year that my American University students and I first added Nagasaki to our study tour in Hiroshima and Kyoto, I asked him what he thought about Harry Truman. He minced no words in expressing his deep disdain for Truman. He expressed no hint of being willing to forgive those responsible for the atomic bombing, which he considered cruel and unjust, even barbaric. He saw nothing positive resulting from the suffering that he and others had undergone and deplored the nuclear sword of Damocles that has hung over all humanity since August 1945. There is nothing nuanced, ambivalent, or qualified about his feelings on this topic. As he writes in his memoirs, "There are people who made the atomic bomb, people who ordered its production, people who ordered its use, and people who rejoiced at its use. I don't regard these people as humans."

Taniguchi spoke to my students almost every August between 1998 and his death. His testimony was powerful. It was also unforgettable. That his presentation to my students focused largely on the 1945-1949 period is completely understandable. He was horribly burned in the bombing of Nagasaki. He was a 16-year old postal worker delivering mail on his bike when the bomb exploded. Burns covered his entire back. He remained bedridden, lying on his stomach, for one year and nine months. The pain was so intense and unrelenting that he begged nurses and doctors to kill him. "Lying on my stomach with my chest wounds pressed down into the bed—the pain was excruciating," he recalled. The bedsores covering his chest, back, sides, jaw, and knees were so deep that portions of his heart and ribs were exposed. He could not move his neck or right arm. Pus poured from his maggot-infested wounds. Though no one expected him to live, he did and on March 20, 1949, three years and seven months after the bombing, he was finally discharged from the hospital.

Marine Sergeant Joe O'Donnell arrived in Nagasaki soon after the bombing with orders to provide a photographic record of the bombing's aftermath. He arrived at the temporary relief hospital at Shinkozen, to which Taniguchi had been moved, on September 15. There he encountered the horribly burned teenager. O'Donnell photographed Taniguchi's burned body. He recalled, "I waved the flies away with a handkerchief, then carefully brushed out the maggots, careful not to touch the boy's skin with my hand. The smell made me sick and my heart ached for his suffering, particularly because he was so young. I decided then that I would not take other pictures of burned victims unless ordered to do so." O'Donnell hid 300 images from U.S. occupation authorities and brought them back to the United States, where he stored them in a trunk for nearly a half century before ginning up the courage to look at them. Even then, he found them so disturbing that he joined the ranks of activists fighting to abolish nuclear weapons.

Meanwhile, despite being in constant pain, Taniguchi tried to resume a normal life. On April 1, 1949, he returned to work. His back, which had not yet completely healed, was covered with scars. His legs and bottom were covered with keloids. He had limited movement in his left arm. The left side of his chest was deeply gouged from the bedsores. As he writes in this memoir, he felt "hatred towards war and the atomic bomb" and "profound anger" toward government authorities and adults in general for the wartime lies that he and others had been fed.

So this is no tale of Christian forgiveness. Taniguchi knew who and what to blame and stated it openly. Among the targets of his anger was the Atomic Bomb Casualty Commission (ABCC), which the U.S. occupation authorities set up in Hiroshima in 1947 and Nagasaki in 1948 not to treat the atomic bomb victims but to study them. Initially curious about the research, he volunteered to be studied. But after being examined, he was told, "No abnormality existed." No abnormality? Incredulous and furious at this "truly merciless human experimentation," he never again set foot at the ABCC. Like so many other Hibakusha, he was outraged over the humiliating treatment he received.

Back at work in the Telegraph Office, he faced discrimination from both management and fellow employees. The better educated and higher paid office workers looked down upon the delivery workers. On one occasion, when Taniguchi and other telegraph delivery workers formed a band to play music at the send-off for a fellow worker who had been drafted, the office workers mocked their poor performance. "They treated us like idiots, and I was so angry," Taniguchi recalled, adding, "We took them to a shrine behind our office and beat them up." Taniguchi was clearly not one to turn the other cheek or behave like a "sacrificial lamb." He joined the labor movement to fight for equal wages, explaining, "I could not stand the discrimination I witnessed against equal human beings." His colleagues, he reported, "often said I had a strong sense of justice or that I had guts." In Taniguchi's case, it was not an either/or. He had both.

But Taniguchi had not yet gotten involved in Japan's fledgling anti-nuclear movement. The Castle Bravo hydrogen bomb tests in March 1954 would change that. The uproar over the nuclear contamination of the crew members aboard the Lucky Dragon No. 5 fishing vessel convinced Taniguchi that the time was right to organize for the abolition of atomic and hydrogen bombs. On October 1, 1955, he, his friend Yamaguchi

Senji, and 14 other atomic bomb survivors who had also had surgery at Nagasaki University founded the Nagasaki A-Bomb Youth Association. From its inception, the association worked closely with the Nagasaki A-Bomb Maidens Association. The two organizations merged in May 1956, forming the Nagasaki A-Bomb Youth and Maidens Association with Yamaguchi as president and Taniguchi as vice-president. The next month, in June 1956, saw the formation of the Nagasaki Council of A-Bomb Survivors (Nagasaki Hisaikyo), which Taniguchi would chair for many years before stepping down in 2017. Hisaikyo often joined forces with Gensuikyo, the Japan Council against A and H Bombs, which had formed in September 1955 from the merger of the Organizing Committee of the World Conference against A and H Bombs and the National Council for the Signature Campaign against A and H Bombs. Japan was abuzz with anti-nuclear activity and Taniguchi was in the forefront of the organizing efforts.

Though active in the anti-nuclear movement, Taniguchi had not yet spoken publicly about his own struggles as a victim of the bombing. In August 1956, he attended the World Conference Against A and H Bombs in Nagasaki. On August 9, Chieko Watanabe addressed the assembly of 3,000 people on behalf of the Youth and Maidens Association. As a 16-year old, Watanabe had been mobilized as a student and was working at the Mitsubishi Electric Manufacturing Company when the bomb exploded. A steel beam fell, breaking her spine and leaving her a paraplegic. For 10 years, she remained secluded in her home until four A-bomb maidens visited her. At the World Conference, her mother carried her to the podium, from which she tearfully pleaded, "Please look at me in this miserable condition. We must be the last victims of atomic bombs. Dear friends from around the world, please work together and abolish all A and H bombs." All, including Taniguchi, were deeply moved. The entire hall, he writes, "exploded with applause." This was particularly moving, he remembered, because "in fear of discrimination and prejudice, the *hibakusha* had kept their mouths shut for a long time."

Taniguchi's opportunity came the next day in front of a smaller workshop. It was a life-changing experience. He writes, with simple elegance, "Words began to pour from my lips as though a dam inside me had broken—what had happened on 'that day,' the three years and seven months of hospitalization, the pain on my back, and the accumulated suffering and resentment. It was the very first time I had spoken in front of a large number of people, and I was not sure if my talk conveyed what I wanted, but I received great applause from the audience."

That day was not only a milestone for Taniguchi, it was a milestone for all Hibakusha, 800 of whom attended the conference. The attendees founded the Japan Confederation of A- and H-Bomb Sufferers Organizations (Nihon Hidankyo), which would go on to lead the fight for Hibakusha medical care and other rights and benefits. Taniguchi would later become a co-chairperson of Hidankyo.

Taniguchi's memoir operates on at least two distinct though tightly intertwined levels. On the one hand, it is the story of his involvement in and leadership of the anti-nuclear movement. In that regard, it provides revealing new insight into the history of the antinuclear movement in Japan. Over the years, Taniguchi worked with virtually all the leading Hibakusha and antinuclear organizations. He saw the squabbles and feuds and played the role of peacemaker, understanding that the common interests and objectives far outweighed the differences and that in unity there was strength. And the movement, he believed, had not gotten the credit it deserves. While the movement has not succeeded in eliminating nuclear weapons as it has striven to do, the Hibakusha, through their prominent and highly visible participation, have helped stigmatize nuclear weapons and convince the world that such weapons should never again be used.

On the other hand, it is the story of the extraordinary challenges Taniguchi faced socially and psychologically to deal with the personal tragedy that almost destroyed his life. Among the challenges that he and so many other Hibakusha faced was dealing with the often disfiguring physical scars that the bombings had caused. In the memoir, Taniguchi describes the persisting sense of shame he felt when people stared at the scars on his face. He tells of his insecurity around women, which was reinforced by being rejected for marriage by five or six different potential partners. He tells of marrying Eiko ten days after meeting her and the trepidation he felt during their honeymoon, fearing she would leave him after seeing his horribly scarred body. They remained happily married for more than 60 years before Eiko passed away in 2016 at age 86.

Taniguchi's sense of shame at being seen in public was eased somewhat by plastic surgery. But the thought of taking his shirt off in public, even at the beach, continued to mortify him. In the summer of 1956, male and female members of the Youth and Maidens Association went by boat to a secluded beach, where, for the first time, they were able to shed their clothes in public without having people stare at them scornfully. Taniguchi recalls, "As *hibakusha* with visible scars, we had been afraid to show our bodies in bathing suits for fear that people would look at us coldly and with disgust." But since they were all Hibakusha, the inhibition was gone. "We were so excited," he writes, "like little children."

The thought of exposing his body in front of non-Hibakusha, however, was still unimaginable to him. Finally, one day, a co-worker urged him to shed his long-sleeve shirt at the beach and he decided he was ready to take the plunge. As he ran topless to the beach, he "knew people were staring at me in surprise but I didn't care. I was crying in my heart, 'Look at me and think about why I became like this. Don't turn your face away.'"

But Taniguchi's life changed dramatically in 1970 when the *Asahi Shimbun* published a photo taken by a U.S. soldier on January 31, 1946 of Taniguchi's raw, red, scarred back as he grimaced in pain. The photo came from 16mm color film footage that had been found in the U.S. National Archives. A week later, the shocking footage was broadcast on Japanese television. Up to that point, Taniguchi had been active in the anti-nuclear movement but had not been a prominent national leader. However, when a British TV crew came to interview him, he removed his shirt and displayed his scarred body. After that, his life would never be the same. He was catapulted into a leadership position and was in constant demand as a speaker. The image of his back became one of the most universally recognized reminders of the horrors of nuclear war and his passionate involvement in both the fight for Hibakusha rights and the nuclear abolition movement have, as he himself and other Hibakusha say, "brought him back to life again" and imbued his life with special meaning.

When Taniguchi addressed my students, as he did with other groups, he held up the large color photo of his raw red back. The photo itself is more than most students can bear. And then he removed his shirt, revealing a heart that could be seen beating through his ribs and a back covered with scars. The natural instinct of the students was to turn away, but, out of respect, they tried to choke back their tears and not avert their gaze, looking at Taniguchi's disfigurement just as he wanted them to and understand more deeply the abomination of nuclear warfare that Taniguchi had been trying to convey.

In these pages, Taniguchi shares his extraordinary life with us. Despite his having undergone dozens of surgeries, undertaken extraordinary daily measures just to stay alive, and endured endless suffering, Taniguchi's story is inspiringly life-affirming. It is the remarkable chronicle of a man who had gone beyond personal tragedy to dedicate himself to the struggle to make sure that life will continue on this planet and that others will never need to suffer the way he has. Taniguchi ends with a simple plea, but it is the one that motivated him for more than 70 years: "Let Nagasaki be the last atomic bombed site; let us be the last victims. Let the voice for the elimination of nuclear weapons spread all over the world." At a time when the threat of nuclear war is the greatest it has been since the Cuban Missile Crisis almost six decades ago, this simple plea carries a poignancy that must be heard. Human beings and nuclear weapons really can no longer co-exist.

March 2020

PREFACE

As Long As My Life Continues

Taniguchi Sumiteru
Co-Chairperson, Japan Confederation of Atomic and
Hydrogen Bomb Sufferers Organizations
(Nihon Hidankyo)

NOW THAT 70 YEARS HAVE passed since that day, there is hardly any time left for us, the *hibakusha* (atomic bomb survivors), to speak about our experiences. When I received a request for interviews from Mr. Hisashi Tomokuni, a reporter at The Nishinippon Shimbun, I decided to accept it, intending to leave behind a farewell note.

On August 9, 1945, an atomic bomb killed many scores of innocent civilians in a moment. With my entire back severely burned, I have sustained permanent scars and pain over the course of my life. As the only country ever to have been attacked with nuclear weapons, Japan once made a pledge, to the war victims and atomic bomb survivors, that it would never start a war again. However, observing the ongoing debates over constitutional revision and the right to collective self-defense, I cannot help but think that Japan is again proceeding headstrong towards war. With the rise of generations that know nothing

Preface

about war or the atomic bombing, it seems that the bitterness of the past is fading from people's minds.

With peace now being eroded, I hope that by following the story of my life, which was derailed by the atomic bomb, you will learn how stupid war is and how terrible nuclear weapons are. Furthermore, please do not forget how people suffered in the past and to this day.

Though the average age of the *hibakusha* now exceeds 78, there is still a long way to go toward achieving the abolition of nuclear weapons and state compensation for the *hibakusha*. I pledge to continue my struggle, as long as my life continues.

FOREWORD

My Wish for This Story to Be Read by as Many People as Possible

Hiroshi Taka
Representative Director, Japan Council against
Atomic and Hydrogen Bombs (Gensuikyo)

FOR THE FIRST TIME, WE have the opportunity to read about the experience of Mr. Taniguchi, the atomic bomb survivor from Nagasaki, and his life thereafter, in his own words.

There is a book featuring Mr. Taniguchi titled "The Postman of Nagasaki" written by the British writer Peter Townsend; however "Having A-Bomb on My Back [*Genbaku wo seotte*]" is told by Mr. Taniguchi himself.

The atomic bombs dropped on Hiroshima and Nagasaki claimed over 210,000 lives by the end of 1945. The victims' suffering is indescribable. Mr. Taniguchi's back was exposed to atomic heat rays at a distance of 1.8km from the epicenter. Thus he no longer has sweat glands on his back, making him unable to sweat in the heat of the summer, and the lack of fat under the skin makes him defenseless against the winter's cold. Furthermore, the rotten under-skin tissue of his chest caused by bedsores has exposed a part of his bone.

The journey he took in deciding to reveal his irradiated body and to tell his story as a survivor is inspiring. The turning point came when Mr. Taniguchi, who feared the public eye and discrimination, was bathing in the sea, and a colleague said to him, "Hey, Sumi-san, take your shirt off!"

Anger building, his passion towards "No More Atomic Bombs" heightening, Mr. Taniguchi became increasingly involved in the anti-atomic and hydrogen bomb movement that was to emerge.

Mr. Taniguchi, disliking exaggeration and dramatization of stories, is a person who is honest about his feelings with himself and others. Therefore his story shows the truth, as well as life's joys and sorrows, which have given him the courage to live his life. One such story took place on his way back from his honeymoon with his new wife Eiko. It thrills, moves, and makes you smile in the end.

I met the journalist Mr. Hisashi, who wrote the original series of newspaper interviews with Mr. Taniguchi, in the spring of 2013. When I first heard about the project, I honestly felt it would be no easy task to create a work that exceeds "The Postman of Nagasaki." However, an exceptional book was produced. Each story stays loyal to the way in which Mr. Taniguchi would have told and felt it, and his expression can almost be seen on the pages.

In August 2015 it has been 70 years since the atomic bombs were dropped on Hiroshima and Nagasaki in 1945. The worldwide concern for the inhumane nature of nuclear weapons has increased, and witnesses to the realities of the bombs are sought after; however, time is limited for those who experienced that day firsthand. I cannot help but wish for this book to be read by as many people as possible.

Additional note in 2020:

The project of publishing the English edition of this book began with the request from Mr. Taniguchi upon the book's first publication in Japan. Many people have contributed to bringing this project into realization in the 75th anniversary of the atomic bombing. We express our special thanks to the following translators, proofreaders and English checkers for their great contribution.

Asato Rieko
Joseph Gerson
Lani Gerson
Hasunuma Yusuke
Hirano Emiko
Izumi Toshikazu
Kataoka Fumiko
Kim Hwami
Kodama Kaoru
Kuroda Ikuyo
Matsuura Tetsuro
Ohno Naomi
Moroi Yuichi
Nakamura Mizuki
Okada Norio
Okamoto Makiko
Okazaki Shushi
Ouchi Hibiki
Ozaki Fuki
Mary Popeo
Sato Ai
Sato Yuki
Mark Selden
Takakusaki Hiroshi
Toyama Kyoko
Sofia Wolman
Yabe Michiko

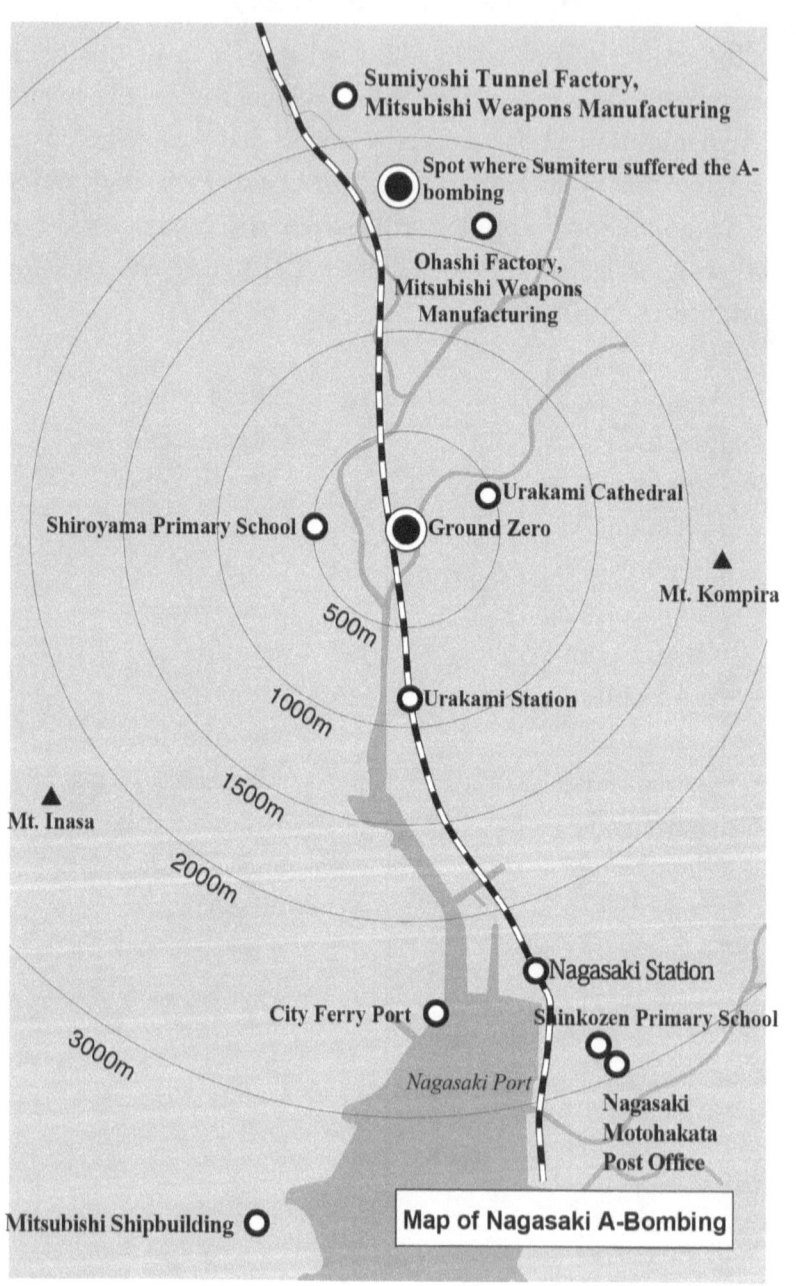

CHAPTER 1:

Struck by the Atomic Bomb: The Beginning of My Endless Agony

Scars on my back still aching

In the Nagasaki Atomic Bomb Museum, there is a picture exhibited of a boy lying on his stomach, his face contorted with pain and the whole surface of his back stained crimson with blood. The boy in the photograph is me at age 17.

On August 9, 1945, an atomic bomb was dropped on Nagasaki. I was delivering the post when heat rays from behind me suddenly burned my entire back. The skin that covers my back now is not normal skin, but a thin membrane called cicatrix. Because the cicatrix does not have sweat or sebaceous glands, calcareous matter – hard lumps like stone – gradually builds up underneath, growing bigger until it finally breaks through the skin.

On any given day, the pain in my back takes many forms. Sometimes it throbs as if I had been struck. Other times I feel a stinging pain like I am being pricked by needles. I cannot lie on my back even on a bed quilt, as this feels as though I am lying on rocks. Controlling my body temperature is also difficult. In the summer, the heat trapped in my body makes me feel burning hot, and in the winter I shiver with cold despite the many jackets I put on.

I am 166 centimeters (5' 4") tall and weigh 47 kilograms (104 pounds). I have been the same weight for a long time. Some people say, "You should eat more." But if I put on any more weight, the cicatrix on my back will be pulled tight and tear open. If I drink alcohol, dilated blood vessels cause me pain. Because I lay on my stomach for one year and nine months after the bombing, the flesh on the left side of my chest became covered in bedsores and rotted away. Between my ribs you can see my heart beating. When I breathe deeply, I feel pain in both my chest and back. Because of this, I cannot speak loudly. For me, to live means to endure agony.

Having experienced the first nuclear war firsthand, and as a *hibakusha* (A-bomb sufferer), I instinctively know the horror of nuclear weapons. The Nagasaki A-bomb is estimated to have killed 73,884 people by the end of 1945. Many were burned to cinders and others died of thirst. Of those who survived the immediate blast, many died later on from the delayed effects of the bomb. Even now, radiation from the bombs gnaws away at the bodies of the *hibakusha*. These weapons of the devil still prevail in the world, numbering some 17,000.

What I am going to tell you now is an account of my life, during which I lived with the A-bomb on my back. It is also a history of the struggles of the *hibakusha*, who have worked to eliminate nuclear weapons and improve *hibakusha* aid policies. More than half a century has passed since that fateful August day, and the agonies of the past seem to be falling into oblivion. I am afraid of such a lapse of memory. I am afraid that the resulting oblivion will lead to the approval of nuclear weapons. Please, don't avert your eyes, but give heed to my story.

When I speak, I always show the photo of myself with my entire back burned by the atomic bomb.

Mother's death shapes my life

In the spring, Umi-no-Nakamichi Marine Park, a state-run park in Higashi-ku, Fukuoka City, busts into beauty with all kinds of flowers. Along with the neighboring aquarium, it is always crowded with tourists. I was born near the park in Saitozaki, Shigashima-mura in former Kasuya-gun on January 26, 1929. I was the third child born to my father Takamori Sadamichi, a locomotive engineer, and my mother Kiku. My father named me Sumiteru, using characters that meant that I would "illuminate every corner, even where lights do not reach."

When my mother died a year and a half later, my life changed course. My father left my elder sister, elder brother, and me with my mother's family and moved to Manchuria (Northeast China) to work with the South Manchuria Railway.

The house of Taniguchi Taga, my grandmother, was halfway up the hill of Inasayama in Nagasaki City, standing isolated in the middle of vegetable fields. My brother and I used to run around the mountain catching white-eyes with birdlime.

Grandma Taga had a companion named Sakutaro who lived in the house with her. I called him Grandpa. After I was hit by the A-bomb, he tended to me and did not leave my side.

Grandma worked hard to support us children and Grandpa, who did not have steady work. She tilled the land and grew vegetables, gathered night soil in town, reared silkworms for cloth, bred chickens to sell to butchers, and even bred guinea pigs to be used at university laboratories. She was a strong-willed, unyielding woman, but she was also kind to everyone. Once we were fed, she used to distribute the remaining vegetables to neighbors.

My daily task was to feed the animals. Every morning I went down the 300 steps overlooking Nagasaki Port to a tofu shop to buy soy pulp for animal feed, and when I came home from Asahi Primary School, I cut grass to feed to the chickens.

In my childhood, I was a bit timid. One day, Grandma asked me to stay home while she went out. I was afraid that someone would come, so I went out to the garden, climbed up a persimmon tree, and hid there for a while. Grandma was furious when she came back and found me in the tree. "How can you mind the house when you're all the way up there?" she roared, and began prodding me with a bamboo stick. I desperately tried to escape, climbing further up the tree.

On the other hand, I was somehow stubborn, too. One day,

I did something naughty at school. A teacher ordered me to stand in the corner of the playground for a while. Then, forgetting that I was there, the teacher went home for the day. That night, a school janitor found me and told me to go home. But I did not move, because I was standing there by the teacher's order. The teacher came back to the school in haste and said to me, "I am sorry." Was I patient? Or simply stubborn? This characteristic remains within me even now.

Nagasaki, a city of military factories

After the Nagasaki Iron Mill, built in 1861 in the closing days of the Tokugawa Shogunate, was sold to Iwasaki Yataro (the founder of Mitsubishi Zaibatsu), the city's development centered on Mitsubishi's Nagasaki Shipyard. During the time of the Sino-Japanese War and then the Russo-Japanese War, Nagasaki, which had once prospered on trade, rapidly transformed into a city of military industries.

Mitsubishi Munitions Works and the Mitsubishi Steel Mill were built in the Urakami District during the Taisho period (1912-1926). Two factories for electrical machinery and shipbuilding followed. These four plants attracted subcontractors and affiliated companies, and schools, hospitals, and dormitories were built. One day, in the skies over this industrial zone sometimes called "Urakami Factory," an atomic bomb would explode.

I lived in Hiratokoya-machi near the Nagasaki Shipyard, where many of the shipyard workers also lived. When I was a pupil in primary school, I heard a rumor that a huge warship was being built, and that a fence was constructed to hide the dock from people on the other side of the port. A man rumored to be one of the battleship's signals officers was living in a rented house nearby in the neighborhood.

I was moved up to an advanced course in Fuchi Elementary School in the spring of 1941, the same year that the Pacific War broke out. Later that year, we held a send-off party in honor of the signals officer and other sailors at our house, as ours was a little bigger than the other houses in the neighborhood. It seemed that the warship had been completed, and would soon set sail. More than 20 other crewmembers also came up to our house, and I hoped that they would do their best for the sake of our country. I still have a picture of the uniformed sailors and myself from that day. Now I realize that the warship was "Musashi," which was built at the Nagasaki Shipyard.

During the early days of the war, the whole town was caught up in fervent enthusiasm as news and expectations of "victory" spread. Yet in school, we still practiced military drills. We lined up side by side, and in response to orders, we stuck out the wooden sticks in our hands single-mindedly, yelling "Ei! Ei!" The drill would continue for about one hour, but was much more fun than the classroom lessons that required brain work. I used to tell my friends that I would love to join the navy soon and become a war pilot.

After I finished the two-year advanced course, I had to get a job. Some friends were going on to continue their schooling, but my family could not afford to send me on in school. My sister, who was six years older than me, and brother, who was two years older than me, had left home and gone out of the prefecture for work. When I thought about my Grandma and Grandpa, I knew I had to get a job to support our family. Through a friend of hers, Grandma found a job for me at the Motohakata Post Office of Nagasaki.

A send-off party held at my house for the crewmen of a battleship built at Mitsubishi's Nagasaki shipbuilding plant

Draft papers delivered at midnight

The Nagasaki District Court stood alongside the Regional Legal Affairs Bureau office in Manzai-machi, Nagasaki City. At one corner of the district, where the Sumitomo Life Insurance building currently stands, stood the Motohakata Post Office. I began to serve there in 1943 at age 14. To commute to the office, I went down the 300 steps from my house, halfway up Inasayama to the harbor, and then took a city ferryboat. Because most of the men had been drafted and there were hardly any male workers left, I was trained mostly by the women workers at the Post Office.

To my dismay, I had to use a bicycle to deliver the mail. Living on a hillside, I had never had the chance to ride a bicycle, and besides, I was so short that when I sat on it my feet could not reach the ground. To get myself onto the bike, I put my full weight on the pedal on one side, and then jumped up and did the same on the other side.

After a month of getting used to riding the bike, I began to really enjoy delivering the mail. My coverage area gradually expanded to include Urakami region, where there were many military factories, the city center, and even suburbs. I went to many different places. At times I carried the bike on my shoulder to walk up a mountain, and tied a string to it and slid it ahead of me on the way down. But I stayed on my bike when crossing shallow water or going down steps. I loved going fast. Among the children along my route and among my colleagues, I was known as the "speed maniac."

I dealt often with a special kind of delivery called an express telegraph. This was a secret document sent from the military to a munitions factory, which we had to deliver within 15 minutes after it had arrived.

One evening, we received an express telegraph addressed to the Ohashi Factory of the Mitsubishi Weaponry Mill, which was the farthest mill from the office. On my way to the mill I felt uneasy, as I knew that a house next to the factory let their two German Shepherds run free at night. As I feared, the dogs began chasing me. If caught I would pay dearly. I was desperate, so I ran into the factory at full speed. Luckily, I was safe, but I was scolded harshly for forgetting to salute the guard.

As the war neared its end, draft cards often came in by telegraph throughout the night. I went door-to-door, delivering dozens of telegraph slips designating the date of induction and the name of the unit the man would join. Neither I nor the person who received the telegraph uttered a word. What a notion, to deliver call-up papers in these late hours! Returning to the office in the light of the morning sun, I felt uneasy about the consequences of where Japan was headed.

August 9, the fateful day

From the first air raid by U.S. forces on August 11, 1944 until the end of the war, the City of Nagasaki suffered a total of five air raids. The number of alerts and air raid warnings increased day by day, and were issued so frequently that we became accustomed to them. They were troublesome for us, because whenever a warning was issued, even at midnight, we had to gather at Motohakata Post Office to guard our mails.

As I said before, I commuted by city ferryboat from the foot of Mt. Inasayama. Oftentimes, it was already midnight, and the city boat was no longer in service by the time the air raid warning was lifted. Today, there is a bridge called Asahi-Ohashi near the Nagasaki Japan Railway Station, but in those days I was unable to go back home unless the boat was in operation, so I often stayed overnight at the office.

On the night of August 8, 1945, I stayed at the office due to an air raid warning. I was supposed to deliver telegrams the following afternoon, but a senior colleague asked me to switch to a morning shift. The Motohakata Post Office was located some three kilometers from what would become the bomb hypocenter. Though the office burned in the fire that broke out several hours after the A-bombing, the casualties were limited. If I had not changed my shift, I would have been safe at the office when the bomb hit.

Early in the morning on August 9, Grandma Taga came to the office to bring me a packed breakfast and lunch. Because of the frequent air raids those days, I told her to go back home as quickly as possible. I had no way of knowing that our next meeting would be three years and seven months later.

I finished the two meals in a few gulps and left the office for the 9 a.m. delivery. I passed through the Urakami industrial district, and as I approached the Nishi-Urakami Post Office, my bicycle tire blew out. I fixed the flat and took a glance at my watch: 11 o'clock in the morning.

I had pedaled about 100 meters when I heard the buzzing of a plane coming from behind. As an air-raid warning had just been lifted, I thought that this was strange and began to turn around. A dazzling flash of light and then a shock wave came from behind me and to the left. Together with my bicycle, I was blown a few meters away. I had no idea what was happening and I tried desperately to stay on the ground, which was roaring and trembling like an earthquake.

When I lifted my head, two children, who were about four or five years old and who often exchanged greetings with me, came into sight, flying by like pieces of dirt. A rock, some 30 centimeters in diameter, came crashing into my hip. I feared that I would die. Lest I should grow faint of heart, I kept telling myself, "I will not die here," and endured.

It was at two minutes past 11 a.m. on August 9, 1945 that, at age 16, I was struck by the atomic bomb about 1.8km (1.1 miles) from the center of the blast. So began my long, unending agonies that continue to this day.

Myself around the time when I started working for the Nagasaki Motohakata Post Office

Escaping from hell

After lying face-down for about three minutes, I mustered my courage and rose to my feet. The world I saw before me had been completely transformed by the blast and heat rays. The house where I had most recently delivered mail remained standing, but all the others were crushed to the ground. The frame and wheels of my red bicycle were totally broken and contorted. I used my arm to touch my back, and realized that my shirt was gone. Something black and slimy stuck to my hand. My left arm was burned, and peeling skin hung down from my fingers and almost to the ground. I collected the mail that was scattered around me into the bag hanging from the handle of my bicycle. It so happened that on that day, I was carrying important registered mail in the pocket of my trousers. "I at least I have to deliver the registered mail," I thought. Making sure the mail was still in my pocket, I began to take steps.

One of the two children whom I had seen blown away by the blast was burnt black. The other was lying dead, though seemingly unscathed. I saw them and plodded along. I did not feel any pain in my back or arms, nor was there any bleeding. All I could think of was where to go for safety. I made my way some 200 meters to Mitsubishi Weaponry's Sumiyoshi tunnel factory where torpedo parts were manufactured.

On my way to the factory, I passed what used to be Mitsubishi Weaponry's two-story wooden women's dormitory, which was now completely shattered. A few people were standing around the site, their hair so frizzed and their faces so swollen that I could not tell whether they were men or women. I heard some cries for help, but did nothing. I was in such an extreme condition.

There were six tunnel factories where components of torpedo parts were manufactured. I went into one of the tunnels and sat at a desk in the office. A woman who was there took a pair of scissors and delicately cut the dangling skin off my left arm, anointing the burns with machine oil. As the short-sleeved shirt I had been wearing was now completely burnt, I was stripped to the waist. My trousers, too, were partly burned and had a hole in the back. With the woman's help, I removed my trousers, gaiters and rubber-soled shoes, leaving only my underpants on.

Guessing that their factory had been targeted, all the workers were moving about in confusion. Someone said, "Another attack will come. We must evacuate," and people began to make their way to the exit on the other side. I, too, tried to stand up, but was no longer able to rise.

A man in the factory helped me. Carrying me on his back, he got me out of the tunnel, where the Akasako Terminal Tram Station is now located. From there, the man climbed a hill and laid me under a tree at the edge of a farm. There were many wounded people lying around me, groaning and crying for water.

Mushroom cloud rising above Nagasaki City on August 9, 1945. Under the mushroom cloud, tens of thousands people perished.

Guarding the mails to the end

As time went by, the groans around me faded. I bunched my rolled trousers, gaiters, and rubber-soled shoes together to use them like a pillow under my face and kept lying on my stomach at the top of the hill. At about two o'clock in the afternoon, a rescue train arrived down below. I heard someone calling out, "All who can move should come down." People who could still walk began to move towards the railways, leaving me behind as I was unable even to budge. There were many, one after another, who collapsed from their wounds on their way down, taking their last breaths in exhaustion.

I was absolutely parched with thirst. Suddenly I saw a green persimmon fruit hanging from a branch within my reach. I somehow managed to get to my feet, but as I tried to hold onto a branch, I lost my balance and collapsed. A bamboo stump pierced into the right side of my hip. Later, it would swell and fester, but at that moment I did not feel any pain. I picked up the persimmon, which had fallen onto ground, and rushed to take a bite of it. It was so terribly bitter!

That evening, a U.S. fighter plane strafed along the slope of the mountain where I was lying. Bullets hit a rock right beside me. Fury rose from the bottom of my heart when I thought that, after this vast destruction, they were still attacking us. The city spread out before my eyes was a sea of fire, of hell. "Are my grandma and grandpa all right?" I was worried about them.

At dawn, people working as relief workers came and distributed rice balls and tea at the foot of the mountain, but they did not come up to the place where I was lying. Thirsty for water, I headed for a nearby farmers house. I crawled down the slope, 7 or 8 meters on my stomach, and when I reached the kitchen I took a dipper of water from a jug and gulped it down.

After resting for a bit, I noticed that the house had leaned due to the blast. In fear of being buried under the house, I crawled out to the foot of a tree in front of the house, and there I fainted.

I would have gone on sleeping, but I was awoken by a man trying to steal the rolled up trousers and gaiters out from under my head. I frantically clung to the clothing because I had important registered mail in my trouser pockets. "Don't take these!" I yelled at the top of my voice, clinging to my belongings. My wristwatch was taken, but I managed to guard the mail with which I was entrusted.

On the morning of the third day, people from a civil defense unit rescued me. They carried me on a door panel. I asked them to stop by Iwaya Post Office, and finally I managed to deliver the registered mail. Without a word, the postmaster put a *yukata*, an informal cotton *kimono*, on my charred back. Relieved that I had finally handed over the mail, I felt myself losing energy.

Bleeding starts on the 6th day

Lying on my stomach, I was carried on the door panel to the Michino-o Railway Station. There, I was placed under the eaves while I waited for a rescue train to arrive. One of the Iwaya Post Office workers kindly fed me a rice ball. Three days had passed since the atomic bomb was dropped, and injured people filled the station.

When the train came, a military man in a white uniform with a sword strapped to his side stepped out. Maybe because he pitied me, he offered me a ship biscuit. It was the finest hardtack I had ever seen, different from the dark-colored, coarse ones we used to eat. I felt rage, seeing that soldiers were eating such fine food.

Grandpa Sakutaro appeared at the station, and I learned that after searching for me since August 9, he happened to stop by Iwaya Post office where he learned where I was. Looking at me, he repeated over and over, "Alright, alright, not very serious." He got on the train with me, asking a man from our neighborhood who was with him to go inform my family about me.

We got off the train at Isahaya Station, and I was carried to Isahaya Elementary School where I was told that I could get treatment. What I received cannot really be called treatment. There were many wounded people, and the deceased were carried out one after another.

On the sixth day after the bombing, I started to feel pain on my back and blood began to seep out from my left arm. The atomic bomb had burned the whole of my back and left arm, the upper part of my right arm, the outer side of my left thigh, the heel of my left foot, and a part of my buttocks. Perhaps there was not enough blood in my body to seep out from all these places.

On August 15, Japan accepted the Potsdam Proclamation. We had lost the war. I heard only noise from the radio. Someone grumbled, "The War is over." I did not feel any particular emotion. I was just wondering when I would die.

Some days later, Grandpa decided that I could not get proper treatment at Isahaya and took me to Nagayo-machi, where we relied on his relatives. Though they were distant relatives whom I had not met before, they generously took great care of me. They burned newspaper, made ashes, mixed it with oil and applied it to my back. They made me porridge from sticky rice and something like tea from persimmon leaves.

After staying in Nagayo-machi until September 10 or so, I was brought back to Nagasaki City. The Shinkozen Elementary school, which was close to the Nagasaki Motohakata Post Office where I had worked, had been turned into an emergency relief hospital. This was the start of my life under medical treatment, which continued into the unforeseeable future.

CHAPTER 2

Life in a Hospital for 3 Years and 7 Months

A can full of raw cow livers

Many doctors and nurses helped to treat injured people at the makeshift hospital at Shinkozen Primary School. The medical staff came from inside and outside of Nagasaki Prefecture, including Nagasaki Medical College, Kyushu Imperial University, and Kumamoto Medical College. There was also a medical team dispatched from the Hario Kaiheidan (sailor corps) based in Sasebo.

I was admitted to the hospital in mid-September, and my treatment began with a blood transfusion, as I had become severely anemic. Although the staff successfully stuck a needle into my arm, the blood was not absorbed into my bloodstream, probably because my internal organs must have been badly affected.

One day, the nurses brought in an 18 liter square can full of cows' livers for me to eat from. The nurses chopped the livers into pieces before my nose and brought them to my mouth piece by piece. It was a terrible meal. The smell was so strong, and the taste was extremely bitter. I heard that people were slaughtering cattle in some areas of Nagasaki City, including Ohato and Tsukimachi, and were supplying the meat to the Allied Occupation forces stationed in the city. Just remembering this meal makes me sick.

The wound on my back was treated with oil and rotten pumpkin until a number of other ointments became available. Dr. Shirabe Raisuke of Nagasaki Medical College and the other staff applied snow-white zinc ointment to my back, which really irritated the wound. Then they began to use Rivanol ointment. The ointment was spread on pieces of gauze, which were put onto my back. Because I had a high fever of more than 40 degrees Celsius every day, these pieces of gauze dried up and stuck to the skin on my back.

In order to unstick the gauze, the medical staff used seawater from the Port of Nagasaki, which they boiled in a drum on the playground of the makeshift hospital. Pouring the water onto my back with a watering can, they ripped the gauze away piece by piece. One day, Dr. Shirabe lifted my body in his arms in order to put me into a washing tub filled with antiseptic. Until then, I had been lying face down on a *futon*, and the moment the doctor lifted me up, my whole upper body shifted backward. The shock and sudden, agonizing pain made me faint. Dr. Shirabe told me this story decades later, and I was taken aback that he had done such a careless thing.

Dr. Shirabe was exposed to the atomic bombing while at the Nagasaki Medical College, 500 to 700 meters from the epicenter. 892 people were killed at the college, but miraculously he survived. I heard the doctor was suffering from after-effects, and despite the loss of two sons, he worked hard to relieve and treat survivors just after the bombing. Later in life, he devoted himself to the study of atomic bomb diseases. He died in 1989 at the age of 89 and was awarded Honorary Citizenship of Nagasaki City.

Transfer to the Omura Naval Hospital

Rendered immobile, I had to remain lying face down on my *futon* even to eat and excrete. I was unable to eat properly, and lying stuck in this position was wearying.

I cannot forget the agonizing pain of the getting hypodermic injections in my thigh. Day after day, over and over, nurses kneaded my skinny thighs covered with warmed towels, as they injected what nowadays would be unthinkable amounts of Ringer's solution under the skin of my thighs with hypodermic needles.

Once, Grandma Taga came to the makeshift hospital at Shinkozen Primary School to see how I was doing. I did not know this at the time. Since then, I learned that the mere sight of me, with my back burnt all over, made her feel sick and collapse. After that, she did not come to see me in the hospital. But Grandpa laid out his *futon* next to me and constantly tended to me. He always said, "Not a big deal." I suppose that with the injured people around me dying one after another, Grandpa was telling that to himself, too.

In mid-October, 1945, our makeshift hospital was closed because the Wartime Damage Protection Law only maintained temporary aid stations for a two-month period. Several other stations in the city were reportedly closed as well. Grandpa was at a loss of what to do when he was told to bring me home. We lived on the side of Mt. Inasayama, and would have to climb the flight of 300 steps to arrive back at home. I was not in a condition to be moved. I lay there helplessly, together with other injured people.

On November 1, nurses came and moved me from my *futon* to a stretcher. I found a black stain about 30 centimeters wide, right under my chest where I had lain. The flesh had begun to decay due to bedsores that had developed from lying in this position since I was admitted to the makeshift hospital. There was another black mark found on the floorboards underneath where my *futon* was laid out. "Radioactivity has dropped down out of his body," the nurses said.

A Red Cross vehicle moved me to Nagasaki Station, where I was put on a train with other patients. It had become dark outside by the time we arrived at the Omura Naval Hospital (known today as the National Hospital Organization Nagasaki Medical Center), which served as a mainstay of treatment for many survivors just after the atomic bombing.

There were many wards in the hospital. I was taken to a room where I was again placed on a bed lying on my stomach. The next morning, I saw persimmons turning orange outside my window. I recalled the years of my childhood, when I had climbed a tree to pick persimmons, and felt deeply that I would never be able to do anything like that ever again.

"Kill me!"

During the war, the whole of Nagasaki Prefecture was used as a naval base. There were munitions factories in Nagasaki City. Sasebo Chinju-Fu (Regional Naval Headquarters) was located in Sasebo City, and a naval air corps was stationed in Omura city. Soldiers wounded on the front were treated at the Omura Naval Hospital.

758 peopled were admitted to the hospital after the atomic bomb was dropped on August 9. It is said that the hospital gave medical treatment to more than one thousand survivors, including those like me who were transferred from temporary aid stations that had closed.

A nurse came to my room the day after I arrived at the naval hospital. Dealing each day with many injured soldiers had made the nurses tough, and they were not particularly kind to me simply because I was a child. At the Shinkozen, the pieces of gauze on my back had been carefully removed after being dampened with seawater, and even though I was only half-conscious, I had felt little pain. But this nurse made no attempt to be gentle as she picked off the gauze with all her force. I screamed out. I felt as though the thin membranes on my back, which had finally begun to cover the wound three months after the atomic bombing, were being stripped off along with the gauze. This was the beginning of my real agony.

The pain was so great that I could not sleep. Furthermore, my back smarted terribly from the ointment that was applied. Every time I heard the rumbling sound of a cart carrying medical instruments approaching, I cried and screamed, "Kill me!" Nurses never kept even a pair of scissors within my reach. If they had, I think that I would have ended my own life. The flesh from my back and chest rotted and oozed down, collecting on the rags laid under my body. Nurses had to replace the soiled rags several times a day.

In the summer, I found maggots crawling inside my left elbow, defying the mosquito net hung around my bed. Eggs hatched one after another. The worms bit in between my bones, causing great pain as if my body were being ground with a rock. I saw grown maggots, but could not remove them because I was rendered immobile.

Nurses always left my medical records at my bedside. The records written in German were impossible for me to read, but sometimes I caught Chinese characters scribbled inside, which read, *"Kitoku Jotai"* (critical condition). Around that time, not a single person expected that I would survive. Every morning, doctors came to see me and whispered, "He is still alive." I learned later that my family was prepared to hold a funeral for me.

Filmed by U.S. investigation team

On January 31, 1946, U.S. soldiers carrying large equipment came into our room, which accommodated six patients. My bed was adjacent to the doorway. I saw some people climbing a utility pole from a connecting corridor to attach a copper wire to an electrical line. Then they drew the wire into our room. The moment the wire was connected to the equipment, bright lights came on. In the days before household wall sockets were used widely, this was the only way to transmit electricity from a utility pole.

The American soldiers, who found me lying on my stomach, captured the image of my back on color film. Unlike today's cameras, low sensitivity cameras in those days required a lot of light. It was a cold day in the middle of winter, but as I lay under the lights, wearing nothing on my upper body, I could not feel cold. 25 years would pass before I saw the image that the American soldiers took of me. With his back covered in fresh blood, a boy contorted his face with pain. This image, captured in film footage and photographs, would come to change my life, but that was a long way off.

The United States Strategic Bombing Survey recorded Nagasaki and Hiroshima on color film in order to study the effects of bombings. I heard that they pressured hospitals to allow them to photograph survivors, using medicine like penicillin as a carrot. Then-hospital director of the Omura Naval Hospital said, "If they want to do so, those worst injured had better be filmed," and a few patients suffering severe injuries/effects, including myself, were chosen. Yamaguchi Senji, an A-bomb survivor later known around the world, was also photographed and recorded, shown seated on a bed with his face and body burnt bright red by the heat rays.

When the atomic bomb detonated, Senji was working as a mobilized student at the foundry of the Nagasaki Mitsubishi Arms Factory, located at the Ohashi Plant 1.1km (0.68 miles) from the hypocenter. His upper body was terribly burned. He was admitted to the Omura Naval Hospital just after the bombing and was discharged in March 1946. When the U.S. forces came to photograph us, Senji walked around the wards together with Yoshida Katsuji (died at age 78 in 2010) and other boys who had been also hospitalized. On the verge of death, I could only listen with envy to the patter of their footsteps and their laughter.

More than seven years later, Senji and I saw each other again. Until then, I had never known whose footsteps I had heard in the corridor while I remained completely immobile on my bed. So initially I thought it was our first time meeting each other. But he had known about me. I suppose he had been curious about me, groaning with pain as I lay face down, with Grandpa tending to me all the time.

It was Yamaguchi Senji, who died at the age of 82 in July 2013, who led me to join the *hibakusha* movement.

Life in Hospital for 3 Years and 7 Months

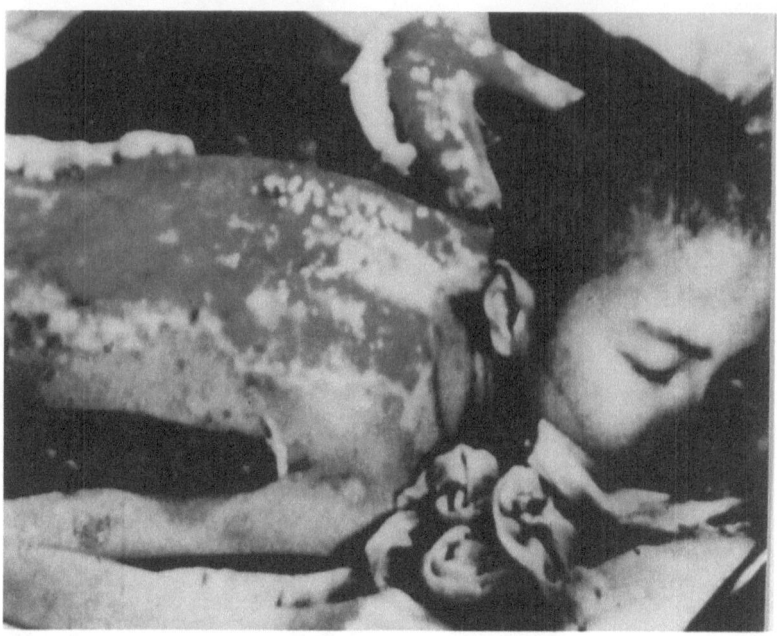

The image in the film shot by the U.S. army would significantly change my life.

My medical record

My hospital chart from my stay at the Omura Naval Hospital is documented in a booklet. The title reads "Genshi-Bakudan Ketsuryo Nisshi" ("Daily Records on Atomic-Bomb Treatment Completion"). "Penicillin poultice; systemic findings worsening, 2.63 million red blood cells/mcls, 11200 white blood cells/mcls…" The chart has detailed medical records like these from November 26, 1945, just after I was admitted to the hospital, to March 20, 1949 when I was discharged. I heard that of the medical records of atomic bomb victims, mine was the only one to survive almost intact.

It was in 1958 that my medical records turned up in the Omura National Hospital that succeeded the Naval Hospital. I had been looking for them in order to file a claim for occupational injury, because I had been injured by the explosion of the atomic bomb while delivering mail. My hospital chart had been left on a shelf in the old, northernmost building on the premises of the hospital.

However, the records of my two most difficult months, between February 27 and April 26, 1946, were missing from the chart. I learned that a research group of U.S. forces, which had studied the effect of the atomic bombing on the human body, had taken them away, together with the records of other patients.

Some people might wonder how I survived despite being in such a grave condition for so long. In fact, the doctors tried several treatments, but none had worked. I remember that there was one particular pill that saved me. This medicine was clearly recorded in my chart.

The Imperial Japanese Army had developed a secret medicine called *"Koha"* (cryptocyanine), and a note written in my chart in June 1946 says, "Temporarily use *Koha.*" After that, I continued to receive Koha treatments, and my medical chart shows that this gradually improved the wound on my back and the level of white blood cells in my body. While the records were written in German, the notes about *Koha* were in Japanese.

A doctor told me that *Koha* was a photosensitive substance, and added that if I did not put it quickly into my mouth, it would disappear. I doubted this was true, and once I hid one of the two administered pills in my hand. After a short time, when I opened my hand, there was nothing there. How amazing!

Four months after I began receiving *Koha*, the wound on my back was less painful. I had been in Omura for about one year, however, I still remained lying face down. One day, a doctor came to my bedside carrying a large mirror and showed me my back for the first time. The size of the wound was bigger than I expected, and I was devastated. But I did find some relief seeing that a thin membrane covered the wound. At that moment, I felt the desire to fight death for the first time.

The bold doctor and I

As my physical condition improved with the use of *Koha*, I tried to move my legs while lying face down. I was not intending to undergo rehabilitation, but I had nothing else to do. This is how I got through each day. In May 1947, for some reason I felt able to stand up. So inch by inch, I slowly turned onto my side and put my feet onto the floor with Grandpa's help.

Because I had been bedridden for one year and nine months, blood rushed down to my toes the moment I stood up. I was dizzy and my feet stung so badly that I could not even identify where they were. When the pain in my feet subsided, I felt fully that finally I could be out of bed. All the doctors and nurses were delighted. Grandpa grew teary-eyed.

The grand surprise was that, despite eating very poorly and having been on the verge of death, I had had a growth spurt and had grown much taller. Grandpa, seemingly relieved to see me walking step by step with a stick, took off for home.

After that, I frequently took walks outside the hospital ward. From those days, I remember Dr. Aso Manabu, who was my attending physician for a full year from April 1948 until I left the hospital. Dr. Aso came from Kyushu University and had entered a national athletic meet as a discus thrower. He was bold and once caught an eel to cook by scooping up water from the pond below the hospital with a washing tub. He cooked rice in a mess tin, and he really seemed to enjoy the eel.

The doctor operated on my left arm. Its skin had been burned by the heat waves and the bone had been left exposed. The elbow was stiffened in the position in which it was bent, so I was unable to stretch it more than 90 degrees. Dr. Aso cut the adhesion with a scalpel, and then transplanted skin from my thighs. Although my left arm could not move the way it used to, I came to be able to stretch it to 110 degrees. My left arm remains this way to this day.

In 2006, I was reunited with Dr. Aso. He contacted me through a TV station after watching a program on which I was featured. Until then I had tried in vain to find the doctor for a long time. Dr. Aso, whom I had given up for dead, now had a different surname, "Asao," having married into his wife's family.

When the doctor saw me for the first time in decades, he was greatly delighted that I was alive. We shared many memories of watching movies or dramas staged by theatrical groups at the hospital. I also asked him to translate my medical records written in German into Japanese.

The doctor spent the last part of his life living with his wife in Yufuin, Oita prefecture. He passed away at the age of 91 in October 2013.

Increasing anxiety before leaving the hospital

My doctor gave me the green light to take a bath for the first time in three years at the end of 1948. I lowered gingerly into a bathtub fearing that the wound on my back might hurt. It did. But as a nurse dried off my body, I felt refreshed. By then, the wound had almost closed, apart from a thumb-sized portion that remained unhealed despite every cure that was tried. In the end, I had to leave the hospital before I was completely cured.

Life in Hospital for 3 Years and 7 Months

At the time of the atomic bombing, the postal service was under the control of the Communications Institute of the national government, and I was a full-time government employee in my position as a mail carrier. My salary was paid even while I was in the hospital, as I had been injured while on duty. Grandpa and Grandma lived on my salary. However, in early 1949, I was surprised to hear from my colleagues who visited me in the hospital about a plan to dismiss me.

I learned later that the *Aka-Gari* [Red Purge] had just begun. For some time after the war ended, the General Headquarters of (the Supreme Commanders for) the Allied Forces (GHQ) developed labor unions under the occupation regime, but soon reversed their policy and began to oppress workers. As the Cold War between the East and the West was beginning, GHQ started to fear that labor movements would join socialist campaigns. *Aka* [red] is an offensive word for Communists. Under the direction of the GHQ, the government and private-sector companies fired Communists and Communist sympathizers. With administrative adjustments also being made, between 10,000 and 30,000 workers were reportedly dismissed from workplaces during this period. Though I had been entirely unaware of what was occurring, the wave of dismissals was about to hit me, too.

I became desperate. Losing my job would make me unable to support my grandparents. "You are still in no shape to work," my doctor said. But I pleaded for and finally got his permission to leave the hospital. I grew anxious as my discharge date neared. Although I could get around, my back was covered with scars. Keloids remained on my legs and bottom. I could not fully move my left elbow. The left side of my chest was gouged due to bedsores, and the left side of my chin and cheek had ulcers. "Can I really work like the others?" "How will people look at me?" Miserable and frustrated, I seated myself on a bench outside my room every night and shed tears.

I also felt hatred towards war and the atomic bomb. We had been told that "Japan will never be defeated!" and that "it is an honor to die for his Imperial Majesty," but I felt profound anger rising up in my mind knowing that such lies had been told of the war. Why didn't adults oppose war? Why did these terrible things have to happen to me?

CHAPTER 3

Adolescent Years That I Declared to Live

Tearful reunion with my grandmother

On March 20, 1949, I was finally discharged from the hospital. Nearly three years and seven months had passed since the bombing, and the sixteen-year-old boy was now a young man of twenty years. I had grown over 30 centimeters and none of my old clothes fit me. I could not go home in my hospital gown so my brother in Osaka sent me a jacket, pants, and underwear. The day I left the hospital, my roommates and nurses saw me off, waving until I disappeared from their sight.

I got on a train at Iwamatsu Station. As I watched the rolling landscape from my window, I vaguely remembered how I had been brought into the train through the window on a stretcher, to be carried to the hospital. As I got closer to Urakami, unfamiliar scenes began to appear in front of me. Everything had been destroyed by the atomic bomb. A series of shacks were lined up in the burned ruins, and everyone there seemed to be in despair.

I finally felt the comfort of home when I arrived at Nagasaki

Station. I walked to a pier at Ohato and crossed the bay over to Asahi-machi Pier by boat. I then had to climb the 300 steps up from the pier to get home. I used to run up to the top of the steps when I was a child, but I could no longer run as before. I stopped and rested many times before finally reaching the top.

When I opened the door, Grandma Taga and Grandpa Sakutaro were waiting for me. "Welcome home," said Grandma with tears in her eyes. It was the first time we had seen each other since we separated on the morning of August 9, 1945. I was so overwhelmed by emotion that I could hardly utter, "I'm home." We celebrated our reunion with a meal, feasting on a whole red snapper with its head and tail, as well as steamed rice with sweet red beans. Grandma and Grandpa talked and laughed a lot. I felt very happy just watching them.

After a while, a group of old women from the neighborhood came to celebrate my recovery. I had not been particularly close with these ladies before, but the relationship among neighbors in those days was much stronger than it is today. They said, "Congratulations on your discharge from the hospital!" and were so happy about my homecoming, as though I were one of their family members. They were drunk and I remember them falling all over me.

I went to the National Omura Hospital a couple times a week for about ten days before I returned to work. The main reason for these visits was to receive a certificate stating my ability to work. At this time I began to wonder about the hospital payments. I never recalled paying for those three and half years at Omura Hospital. Neither Grandma nor Grandpa knew who had paid for it, and even to this day I have no idea. Maybe the hospital paid for it out of their budget.

An anxious day - I returned to work

April 1, 1949 was my first day back at work. I had not been sleeping well since I was discharged from the hospital. My uniform covered the scar on my back, but I couldn't completely hide the scar on my arms in my summer clothes. The marks from bedsores remained on my chin and cheek. I was coming of age and I was very self-conscious about how girls would look at me.

I returned to work full of anxiety. My workplace in the Manzai-machi neighborhood of Nagasaki City was much the same, except my department had been changed. During the war, the postal and telegram services had been managed under the post office, but they were separated now. My position was moved to the telegram department, but was still in the same building. In June 1949, the Ministry of Communications that had exercised jurisdiction over mail and communications was replaced by the newly created Ministry of Posts and Ministry of Telecommunications.

Although I was full of anxiety and tension, everybody gave me a warm welcome. Most members of the department were new to me, as many of my colleagues had died in the bombing, but nobody talked about me behind my back. I felt relieved. My boss was concerned about my physical condition and suggested that I should do office work, but I volunteered to work doing deliveries. Part of my reason for doing this was that I could not sit straight while leaning on a backrest due to the injuries and pain on my back. And I knew that I would become depressed if I sat all day long.

After putting on the uniform, cap, and shoes that my employer provided, I straddled a bike for the first time in a long time. The roads seemed different than they were before the atomic bombing and so did the people in the neighborhood. I struggled to remember the directions to my delivery destinations, but to my surprise, riding a bike was much more pleasant than walking. Nevertheless, I could not help but feel fatigued, and by the time I left work to go home, I had lost my physical stamina. Every time I felt depressed, I told myself, "I survived hell. Now I will show how I can persevere and do the work better than others."

In November 1949, a city-run bicycle racetrack was built in Urakami-Komaba-machi (currently Matsuyama-machi) and bicycle racing became a popular attraction. There were many races among different telegraph offices. I participated with my colleagues in a few of them. The race was for our office's honor. Despite my physical condition, I biked hard, for I had no option but to win. I remember there was a military veteran in our team, who was absolutely faster than anybody else. Sure enough, he later became a professional cyclist.

I got along with my colleagues. All of them are dead now, but we used to play catch in the yard at work and go on overnight trips to Unzen. The fun times I had with my colleagues made me forget about the scars on my back and my worries about the future.

With my colleagues at work before making a delivery
(I am the third person from the left)

Anger towards ABCC

I noticed something odd one day when I was delivering telegrams by bicycle. A Jeep stopped in front of a house and drove some residents away. I asked around and found out that the Atomic Bomb Casualty Commission (ABCC) was doing research on the atomic bomb survivors.

Interestingly, I had not been asked yet. I was curious about this research, so I contacted the ABCC myself and volunteered to participate. In the facility where I was taken, I was stripped and had my blood drawn. After a month of waiting, I received a paper from the commission that simply read, "No abnormality detected."

The scar on my back from the heat rays and radiation had not healed completely, and I was in constant pain. I could not stretch my left arm more than 110 degrees and I often suffered from fatigue. "How can you say that I have no abnormality?" I became so angry after receiving this message. After that, I never returned to the ABCC.

The atomic bomb caused damage in three ways: blast pressure, heat rays, and radiation. Exploding in the sky 500 meters above the epicenter, the atomic bomb created a huge fireball of a few hundred thousand degrees. The blast, heat rays, and radiation produced simultaneously brought most people within one kilometer from the epicenter to an instant death. The impact of the bomb is not over yet, as we, who survived, are still suffering from various medical conditions such as leukemia and increased rates of cancer. The lifelong effect of radiation exposure continues to this day.

The ABCC was established in 1947 by order of United States President Truman to research the impact of radiation on the human body, which was unknown at that time. The U.S.

government, which dropped the atomic bombs on Hiroshima and Nagasaki, did not provide any treatment to the survivors from whom they collected data. I understand that the ABCC did not disclose the results of the survivors' evaluations until the U.S. occupation ended in 1952. The public began to develop hostility towards them, saying, "The ABCC is treating *hibakusha* like guinea pigs."

In 1975, the ABCC was renamed and restructured as the Radiation Effects Research Foundation (RERF), a Cooperative Japan-U.S. Research Organization. It is jointly operated and funded by Japan and the U.S. They claim the purpose of establishing such an organization is "to conduct research and studies…on medical effects of radiation and associated diseases in humans, with a view to contributing to maintenance of the health and welfare of the atomic bomb (A-bomb) survivors…" The organization has tracked more than 120,000 survivors since its inception. I'm told that the results of their research have led to the establishment of international standards for radiation protection.

The necessity of the research institute is understandable to some extent. But why should the *hibakusha* cooperate with them after enduring so much suffering? What the ABCC did was truly merciless human experimentation. It is important not to forget that there are still *hibakusha* who feel humiliated by the way they were treated.

Heartbreak and attempted suicide

If you stand on the Hado Cape in Karatsu City, Saga Prefecture, you can see Fukuoka Prefecture on the other side of Genkai-nada Sea. Today, this place is equipped with an underwater observatory and has become a tourist attraction, but there use to be nothing there. I remember standing on that beach a few years after I returned to work. I was thinking about taking my life.

Around the time that I returned to my job and developed a good command of my work, my Grandpa arranged a number of marriage meetings, but many women rejected me. I had scars all over my body, and I could die at any time. Many *hibakusha* around me were bedridden with diseases from unknown causes. There were cases when people who looked healthy suddenly passed away. People were prejudiced and discriminated against *hibakusha*.

Like many other *hibakusha*, I suffered from anxiety and had an inferiority complex because of the scars on my back and body. I almost gave up on marriage, but somehow I came to date a woman whom I met during my delivery circuit. She, too, was a *hibakusha*. We enjoyed going to movies and eating at a small restaurant together. We talked about trivial things but avoided discussing the future. I was afraid of being rejected again.

After two years of dating, we decided to break up. Our families and friends opposed the idea of our marriage. They told us, "You won't be happy as a married couple." It was tough. I was able to distract myself at work, but whenever I had trouble sleeping due to the pain on my back, my mind kept coming back to heartache and worry. Utterly despondent, I spent all the money I had saved for my wedding on repairing our house, which had been impacted by the bomb. "What are you going to do when you need money for your wedding?" said my grandmother furiously. But I thought there was no reason to save money anymore.

Around this time, I felt increasingly that there was no reason for me to live. I took leave from work for a week without telling anybody. I wanted to see my sister before I died, so I headed to her house in Karatsu. After spending a few nights there, I chose Hado Cape, where I could see as far as Fukuoka, my birthplace, as the place I would die.

As I sat down on a rock, looking at my hometown across the Genkai-nada Sea, the faces of my colleagues and other victims I saw the day of the bombing began to surface. Why was I kept alive? I could not find the answer, but in that moment I decided to outlive the tens of thousands of people whose lives were cut short. That day was the starting point of my commitment and dedication to the *hibakusha* movement for the rest of my life.

Fighting against discrimination

After I decided to live, I was all the more driven to work. But the harder I worked, the more noticeable the discrimination at the Telegraph Office became.

Discrimination was nothing new, and it had existed since the wartime. Those with higher education got office jobs, and those who did not have an opportunity to pursue education were assigned to outdoor labor such as deliveries. The office workers always looked down on us and harshly corrected our manner of speaking.

I still remember a time when one of the senior staff in the delivery department was about to be drafted. In preparation to send off our colleague, my coworkers and I formed a band and began to practice a piece. Some office workers obnoxiously told us how poorly we were playing. They treated us like idiots, and I was so angry. We took them to a shrine behind our office and beat them up. Later, we were scolded severely by our boss.

After the war, the harassment wasn't quite as blatant, but the deliverymen's wage was clearly less than that of the desk workers'. Naturally, it was during that time that I became more involved in the labor movement. Once I even butted heads with the management. As the manager defended his "equal treatment" of all workers, I insisted on a discussion about unequal wages. I could not stand the discrimination I witnessed against equal human beings.

My colleagues often said that I had a strong sense of justice or that I had guts. I refused to do anything unjust and always spoke up when I witnessed unfairness. But I wasn't born with these characteristics. I developed this conviction through my long suffering, so painful it felt as if my flesh and bones had been gouged. It was another manifestation of my anger towards the adults who could not stop the war.

Slowly, I became involved in the peace movement, and my colleagues at my work accepted this warmly. Because of my experience with the atomic bomb, they knew my involvement was true and sincere.

I'm getting a little ahead of myself, but I also began to see the similarities between the peace and labor movements. Around 1959 and 1960, an anti-government struggle spread across Japan over the planned revision of the Japan-US Security Treaty. When there is discrimination, conflict is not far behind. The two movements actually share the same goal: to remove discrimination and work peacefully against wars.

I finally take off my shirt

When I walked outside, I noticed that upon seeing me, women would look surprised and stop to whisper. "They are talking about me again," I thought. As I mentioned before, I had developed ulcers on my chin and left cheek from bedsores because I was bedridden with my face down for one year and nine months. I also had a keloid on my left ear. Unlike the scars on my back and chest, there was no way to hide those on my face. I hated being stared at in public.

Many *hibakusha* suffered from keloid scars. Mr. Yamaguchi Senji, who was also treated at Omura Naval Hospital, was one of them. Senji-san was two school-years younger than I. He had severe keloids on his face and the children in his neighborhood used to call him "Red demon!" He attempted suicide when he was young, just like me. Many *hibakusha* took their own lives, wishing to be free from the pain and anxiety of thinking about their future.

Some doctors started to conduct free plastic surgeries for *hibakusha* to lighten their burden. Professor Shirabe Raisuke of the School of Medicine of Nagasaki University, who treated me at the Shinkozen Special Aid Station, was one such doctor. The medical cost of the surgeries was financed not by the government, but by people's donations and fundraising. In 1951, I underwent surgery to remove the swelling on my face. As the doctor tried to remove the stitches, he also pulled the skin on my face. Dr. Shirabe had to press my face down and pull out the thread by force. When I looked into a mirror after the surgery, I thought that my face looked much better.

Once I felt better about how my face looked, my anxiety shifted towards my back. I often went to the beach with my co-workers during the summer but I always kept my long-sleeve shirt on. I had told them about my scars but I did not feel comfortable taking my shirt off. I was self-conscious that other people were watching, and I did not want to attract attention in public.

One day, we went to Tobo Beach in eastern Nagasaki. The sea was shallow and the beach was famous for its white sand and green pine trees. As I was sitting on the sandy beach, watching other young people having fun, one of my co-workers said, "Sumi-san, why don't you take off your shirt?" In that moment, his words dispelled my long-held hesitation. Before I knew it, I was up, taking off my shirt and running towards the sea. I knew people were looking at me in surprise but I didn't care. I was crying in my heart, "Look at me and think about why I became like this. Don't turn your face away."

"Never again atomic bomb" -- just as I was feeling a growing sense of this affirmation and becoming more outward in my conviction, I met Yamaguchi Senji. This was when the *hibakusha* movement was in its earliest stage.

I took off my shirt on the beach of Tobo

CHAPTER 4

Fear of Nuclear Weapons Enters the Spotlight

The Lucky Dragon No. 5 is exposed to H-bomb fallout

I believe it was in 1954 that a man stopped me on the street while I was delivering telegraph messages near Nagasaki University's School of Medicine. It was Mr. Yamaguchi Senji. This was my first time meeting him, but he had seen me lying in bed while we were both staying at the Omura Naval Hospital.

Senji-san ran a sweets shop in front of the School of Medicine. He had been hospitalized for keloid surgery at Nagasaki University Hospital from the autumn of 1953 to the spring of 1954. Upon a suggestion by Professor Shirabe Raisuke, Senji-san formed an association of patients to follow up with them and observe their recovery processes after surgery. I think he approached me for this reason, and we spoke about our recent situations and health conditions. This patients association laid the foundation for the Nagasaki A-Bomb Youth Association that would be formed later.

I did not know this then, but around the time I met Senji-san, the Japanese people were beginning to more seriously consider the threat of nuclear weapons. This came as a result of the U.S. hydrogen bomb test called Castle Bravo on Bikini Atoll of the Marshall Islands on March 1, 1954. The Lucky Dragon No. 5 [*Daigo Fukuryu Maru*], a tuna fishing vessel from Yaizu City in Shizuoka Prefecture, was exposed to radioactive fallout from the test during its voyage, and one of its crewmembers, Mr. Kuboyama Aikichi passed away 6 months later.

Nine years had passed since the A-bombing. The *hibakusha* already knew the horror of nuclear weapons, but those outside of Hiroshima and Nagasaki did not. I think that there were two reasons for this.

First, post-WWII Japan operated under the Press Code imposed by the occupation forces. Before the San Francisco Peace Treaty came into effect in 1952 and Japan regained sovereignty, the General Headquarters of the Supreme Commander for the Allied Powers (GHQ) governed Japan. Media was censored, and criticism of the GHQ as well as reports, writing, and literature about the A-bombings were banned. In addition, research by Japanese scientists was restricted. The damage caused by the atomic bombing was covered up, which significantly impeded medical research on the aftereffects. With no way to treat their diseases, many *hibakusha* died of unknown causes one after another.

The other reason is that in the years following the atomic bombings, *hibakusha* were struggling to simply live their lives, and could not afford to raise their voices in protest or calls for support. Many *hibakusha* were badly injured, had lost their families, and could not find employment because of their weakened bodies. Their symptoms had no medical explanation at that time. The *hibakusha* suffered from discrimination and prejudice in employment and marriage, and as a result were led to keep their mouths shut.

But after the explosion on Bikini, we gradually rose up to join in the movement against A and H bombs. The first voice of the movement was raised from a place we had never expected: the Suginami Ward in Tokyo.

From Suginami, the movement spread nationwide

The effects of the Bikini Incident in March 1954 went beyond the health problems of the Lucky Dragon No. 5 crewmembers, who were exposed to enormous amounts of radiation from the explosion. A high level of radiation was also detected in their tuna catch. The fear of radiation so close to home drove the housewives of Suginami Ward in Tokyo to take action.

The first people to take action were those involved in the fishing industry. As the Bikini Incident was broadcasted widely, bid prices for fish, including tuna at the Tsukiji Fish Market of Tokyo, plummeted. Rumors and whisperings of "atomic tuna" caused many fish stores and sushi restaurants to close their businesses during that time. Owners of fish stores petitioned the mayor of Suginami for a ban on hydrogen bomb tests and for damage compensation. On April 17, the Suginami Ward Assembly voted unanimously for "a ban on hydrogen bomb tests."

Against this background, a women's group took the lead in forming the Suginami Association for the Signature Campaign against Hydrogen Bombs in May at the Suginami Community Center. Housewives went door-to-door asking people to sign the petition for "a ban on production, use, or testing of A and H bombs." One month later, 265,000 signatures had been collected, the equivalent of almost 70 percent of Suginami's population.

The signature campaign spilled over into other wards in Tokyo and spread rapidly around the country. In August, responding to a call by Mr. Yasui Kaoru, the director of the Suginami Community Center and also professor at Hosei University, the National Council for the Signature Campaign against A and H Bombs was formed. The headquarters was set up in his office. By November 1955, some 32,590,000 signatures had been collected, a number that is hard to imagine today.

Nagasaki had a thriving fishing industry, but I heard it too experienced a drop in fish prices in their Kanto and Kansai area markets. In May 1954, the prefectural teachers' union and others began collecting signatures calling for the ban. However, I don't think that the movement against A and H bombs was very strong in Nagasaki then, and at the time I did not know about the Bikini Incident or the signature campaigns.

As I mentioned, people outside of Hiroshima and Nagasaki were not aware of the aftermath of the A-bombings, and the *hibakusha* were struggling each day to survive while suffering from diseases and aftereffects without any compensation. On the other hand, the members of the Lucky Dragon No. 5 crew were receiving free medical treatment as well as consolatory payments from the U.S. government. The *hibakusha* from Hiroshima and Nagasaki felt abandoned and disappointed because of this, and so they stayed away from the movements against A and H bombs.

The First World Conference against Atomic and Hydrogen

Bombs in August 1955 marked the first involvement of Nagasaki and Hiroshima in these movements. The *hibakusha* finally started to tell their A-bomb experiences, left unspoken for many years.

The World Conference against A and H Bombs

As the Suginami housewives' signature campaign quickly spread, and driven by a groundswell of public opinion across Japan, the National Council for the Signature Campaign against A and H Bombs decided to convene the first World Conference against A and H Bombs.

The World Conference was held in August 1955 in Hiroshima. The city was chosen to address a concern shared among the people of Hiroshima, including Mr. Fujii Heiichi. He claimed, "The movement against A and H bombs lack[ed] the presence of the *hibakusha* and the purpose to relieve their pain." While Mr. Fujii himself was not a *hibakusha*, he had lost his father and sister to the A-bombing and was a leading figure calling on the government to compensate *hibakusha*. Later he became the first Secretary General of Nihon Hidankyo [the Japan Confederation of A-and H-Bomb Sufferers Organizations] and I learned a lot from him over time.

Delegates from 46 prefectures attended the World Conference, as did a wide variety of organizations such as labor unions, women's groups, religious and cultural organizations, and 52 overseas delegates from 14 countries. A total of over 5,000 people participated in the conference. The declaration of the conference, adopted on the final day, put *hibakusha* compensation at the center of the movement against A and H bombs for the first time, stating that, "the unfortunate reality of the victims of A and H Bombs must be widely known in the world. Their relief should be expedited through a global relief movement."

One of the speakers in the conference was Ms. Yamaguchi Misako from Nagasaki, one of the "A-bomb Maidens." She said, "I was 15 at the time of the atomic bombing, and I lost my mother and younger brother. Since that day, for the last ten years, I have spent every day in great pain. I don't remember how many times I wanted to die. But if we die, who would tell the world about our suffering?" It was her first time sharing her story, and it was also the first time that the people in the audience heard the testimony of a *hibakusha*. I heard that those who listened couldn't hold back their tears as she spoke, also crying.

The *hibakusha* who attended the World Conference started building solidarity with one another throughout many parts of Japan. I was also going to be involved in the big change as well. Misako and others invited Yamaguchi Senji to join them for a gathering against A and H bombs to be held in Nagano prefecture that same month. At the event, Senji-san unleashed his pent-up sorrows and pains and experienced the same appreciation, passion, sympathy, and inspiration that the "A-bomb Maidens" had experienced in the Hiroshima conference. Back in Nagasaki, Senji-san said to me, "Let's work in the movement against A and H bombs." In order to oppose the atomic bombs that continued to afflict me, I agreed. Senji, myself, and 14 others from the A-bomb patients association, all of whom had surgeries at Nagasaki University, founded the Nagasaki A-Bomb Youth Association on October 1, 1955.

First World Conference against A and H Bombs held in Hiroshima

"Marriage" of the Youth and Maidens

The Nagasaki A-Bomb Maidens Association was active before the founding of the Nagasaki A-Bomb Youth Association. Girls who were members of the Maidens Association gathered together at the house of Ms. Watanabe Chieko (died 1993 at age 64) who was rendered paraplegic by the A-bomb. They unburdened themselves to each other about their problems with love and marriage. Some members of the Maidens Association also shared their stories at the World Conference against A and H Bombs in Hiroshima.

The Maidens Association began to issue a publication called the *Genbaku Dayori* (A-Bomb Newsletter) on July 20, 1955, just before the World Conference. Although it was a simple newsletter mimeographed on coarse paper, they distributed copies to residents associations in the community and called for support. The editor wrote in the first issue,

"For the past ten years, we have continued to suffer agonies and problems that we haven't told people about, such as our keloids, diseases, marriage, and a self-imposed withdrawal from the society due to the shame we felt as *hibakusha*. Before we knew it, we developed something like a disease wordlessness. But now we finally see that blaming society for its lack of understanding does not help anything. We would like to make a fresh start by issuing *Genbaku Dayori*."

From its conception in October 1955, our Nagasaki A-Bomb Youth Association worked together with the Maidens, and the fourth issue of *Genbaku Dayori*, released on October 10, reported the founding of the Youth Association. Members gathered at Chieko-san's house by night and talked about their jobs, marriages, and the movement for the elimination of A and H bombs.

As we spent time together, it was natural for the Youth Association and the Maidens to consider joining forces. In May 1956, the Youth Association and the Maidens Association merged together and became the Nagasaki A-Bomb Youth and Maidens Association. Newspapers reported the "marriage" of the two organizations, with Yamaguchi Senji as president, and myself as vice-president. I remember that the boys joked, "Young men are going into the maidens" and shared laughter. After this, *Genbaku Dayori* changed its name to *Nagasaki* and was issued for about ten more years.

In the summer of 1956, members of the Nagasaki A-Bomb Youth and Maidens Association went by boat to a secluded beach, thanks to the help and support of the local youth group and women's association of Mogi-machi (located in the suburb of Nagasaki City). As *hibakusha* with visible scars, we had been afraid to show our bodies in bathing suits for fear that people would look at us coldly and with disgust. But since we were all *hibakusha*, there was no reason to hesitate. We were so excited, like little children. The members' smiling faces that day were captured in a picture, although I am not in it because I had to leave early to go to work.

Founding of the Nagasaki Council of A-Bomb Survivors (Nagasaki Hisaikyo)

In September 1955, one month after the World Conference against A and H Bombs, the National Council for the Signature Campaign against A and H Bombs and the Organizing Committee for the World Conference were integrated, and the Japan Council against A and H Bombs (Gensuikyo) was established in order to organize future conferences. Gensuikyo decided at its general meeting in March 1956 to convene the second World Conference. There were three candidates for the conference site: Nagasaki, Hiroshima, and Tokyo.

Before the merging of the Nagasaki A-Bomb Youth Association and the Maidens Association, the two groups worked hard to bring the World Conference to Nagasaki. Yamaguchi Senji and I attended a board meeting of Nagasaki Gensuikyo, founded in November 1955, and appealed for the conference to convene in Nagasaki. At that time, Nagasaki Gensuikyo consisted of a wide variety of members from 24 organizations such as women's groups, youth organizations, parent-teacher associations, and local labor unions, and included prefectural and city assembly members and welfare officers. The campaign to host the conference in Nagasaki became very popular among all the people in Nagasaki City.

Fear of Nuclear Weapons Enters the Spotlight

In May 1956, Nagasaki was announced as the official site for the conference. While preparing for the conference, an A-bomb sufferers' organization was formed by people from a variety of backgrounds.

Among the 12 founding members of the organization were members of the Nagasaki A-Bomb Youth and Maidens Association, including Senji-san, Mr. Sugimoto Kamekichi and Kosaka Hachiro of Nagasaki City Assembly, and Mr. Kino Fumio, head of the City Assembly Secretariat. They wrote, "we call for an A-bomb survivors organization to be established, with the goal of forging the unity necessary to achieve state compensation for *hibakusha*." Copies of the appeal were distributed to every house around Nagasaki's ground zero area.

On June 23, 1956, about 1,000 people gathered at the Nagasaki International Cultural Hall for the founding of the organization. People put aside their political and social differences to take action, sharing their determination to prevent the outbreak of another war and to ensure that we would never be the victims of nuclear weapons again.

Mr. Sugimoto Kamekichi presided as the first Chair, with Mr. Koda Matsuichi as Vice Chair. The founding assembly adopted a three-point resolution calling for the development of the movement against A and H bombs, the promotion of government-funded medical treatment and self-reliance for *hibakusha*, and compensation and support for bereaved families of *hibakusha*. This was the beginning of the Nagasaki Council of A-Bomb Survivors (Nagasaki Hisaikyo), which is the organization that I chair today.

I could not attend the first meeting of Hisaikyo due to my job as a telegraph messenger, but I did go to the Hall to deliver congratulatory messages to Hisaikyo. The moment I went in, passion and excitement hit me. *Hibakusha* whose suffering had been ignored by the government and society for 11 years since the bombing were finally able to band together and voice their demands in public.

I remember having to tear myself away from the Hall to go back to work.

Hibakusha begin to speak out

As the Second World Conference against A and H Bombs in Nagasaki drew near, the city had a welcoming atmosphere. Posters and banners were displayed in shopping streets, while welcome messages were printed on department store wrapping paper. The members of the Nagasaki A-Bomb Youth and Maidens Association were also excited and took to the streets to publicize the event and call for donations.

While preparing for the World Conference, our association worked on the publication of a booklet titled, "We Want No More," which compiled *hibakusha* testimonies. We wanted to convey the feelings that we as *hibakusha* had lived with since that fateful day to the people who would gather in Nagasaki from around the country for the occasion. Our members visited hospitals, schools, and offices to ask survivors to write about their experiences. At a time when *hibakusha* suffered from groundless discrimination and prejudice, it must have taken a great deal of courage for them to publicly identify themselves. 37 *hibakusha* contributed to the booklet.

Did I also write my own story? No, I did not. As I had finished only primary school, I felt that my writing was too poor for essays. I had never told my experience in detail, even verbally. Back then, I was busy with my postal work, and I thought that it was my duty to support our association's activities behind the scenes. It was not until later that I was placed at the center stage of our movement.

The long awaited World Conference against A and H Bombs began in Nagasaki on August 9, 1956. As I was on duty that day, I could not attend the conference, but I could feel the enthusiasm that filled Nagasaki.

Three thousand people from abroad and from across Japan filled the gymnasium of Nagasaki Higashi High School, the venue of the World Conference. Ms. Watanabe Chieko spoke in the opening plenary on behalf of the Youth and Maidens Association. At age 16, Chieko-san was a mobilized student worker at the Mitsubishi Electric Manufacturing Company, located 2.5km (1.5 miles) from ground zero. The explosion of the atomic bomb caused the factory building to collapse and Chieko-san's vertebrae were broken under steel beams, which left her permanently paraplegic. Chieko-san had been shut in at home for ten years after the bombing until four A-bomb maidens came to visit her.

Carried in her mother's arms, Chieko-san tearfully appealed from the podium, "Please look at me in this miserable condition. We must be the last victims of atomic bombs. Dear friends from around the world, please work together and abolish all A and H bombs." Chieko's presence and appeal had a powerful impact on everyone, and the entire hall exploded with applause.

I was overcome with excitement when I arrived at the hall to deliver congratulatory telegrams to the conference. In fear of discrimination and prejudice, the *hibakusha* had kept their mouths shut for a long time. But now many people were coming from all over Japan and from abroad to listen to their appeals and to unite in their commitment to the abolition of nuclear weapons. This made me realize how important it was to put the horrors of the A-bomb into words.

(Photo: Japan Council against A and H Bombs)

Watanabe Chieko (center) speaking at the Second World Conference against A and H Bombs, carried in her mother's arms

Message to the World

My turn to speak came on August 10, 1956, on the second day

of the World Conference against A and H Bombs. I spoke of my A-bomb experience in front of about 100 workers of telegraph and telephone offices from around the country during one of the occupation-based workshops held at the Nagasaki Chamber of Commerce and Industry, a brick building used as an annex of the Nagasaki City Office.

Words began to pour from my lips as though a dam inside me had broken – what had happened on "that day," the three years and seven months of hospitalization, the pain on my back, and the accumulated suffering and resentment. It was the very first time I had spoken in front of a large number of people, and I was not sure if my talk conveyed what I wanted, but I received great applause from the audience.

This turned out to be a historic day for the *hibakusha*. About 800 *hibakusha* from across Japan gathered at the Nagasaki International Cultural Hall and founded the Japan Confederation of A-and H-Bomb Sufferers Organizations (Nihon Hidankyo), the national organization of *hibakusha* groups. Mr. Sugimoto Kamekichi and Mr. Kosasa Hachiro of Nagasaki and Mr. Suzuki Kanichi and Mr. Moritaki Ichiro of Hiroshima were elected as the first co-chairpersons, and Mr. Fujii Heiichi assumed the office of the Secretary General.

Around that time, in addition to those in Nagasaki and Hiroshima, prefectural-level *hibakusha* organizations had been formed only in Fukuoka, Tokyo, and Nagano. Many *hibakusha* living in other parts of Japan had not yet raised their voices. The founding of the *hibakushas'* national organization must have given great encouragement to *hibakusha* scattered around in the country. In fact, after Nihon Hidankyo was born, *hibakusha* organizations popped up one after another in different regions and joined Nihon Hidankyo.

At the founding meeting of Nihon Hidankyo, Mr. Moritaki, then a professor at Hiroshima University, recited the founding declaration, the "Message to the World." He said, "We, who were not killed at that unforgettable moment, finally sat ourselves up and came to this first nationwide conference" and shared the *hibakushas'* pledge to the world, saying, "We must make our appeal to the world. We must demand from our nation what we need. And we must stand up. These conversations provide the occasion to consider the actions we should take to save ourselves."

He also declared, "We have resolved to save humanity from its crisis through sharing the lessons learned from our experiences, while at the same time saving ourselves." We continued to uphold the fundamental demands of the *hibakusha* that were established at that time: "state compensation for atomic bomb damage" and the "abolition of nuclear weapons."

In September 1956, the first meeting of prefectural representatives and board members of Hidankyo was held to examine the draft outline of the *Hibakusha* Aid Law. Hidankyo decided to press for five demands, including full state coverage of the *hibakushas'* medical bills, the *hibakushas'* health management, condolence payment for the deaths, and the establishment of a pension system for the bereaved families. Nihon Hidankyo began to work with Gensuikyo to press the government to enact the comprehensive *Hibakusha* Aid Law. The Act for Atomic Bomb Sufferers' Medical Care was not enacted until April 1957.

(Photo: Rengo Tsushin)

The founding meeting of the Japan Confederation of A- and H-Bomb Sufferers Organizations (Nihon Hidankyo) held at Nagasaki International Cultural Hall

Hibakusha movement bears fruit

> *I have gotten fed up with everything*
> *Gigantic peace statue stands in the A-bomb field*
> *Yes it's alright, it's alright but*
> *The money could have been spent otherwise*
> *"Stone statue cannot ease our hunger"*
> *Please don't call us sordid*
> *It's an honest feeling of us victims*
> *Having kept ourselves barely alive for these 10 years*

This poem, titled "Monologue," was written in August 1955 by Ms. Fukuda Sumako, an A-bomb poet (died in 1974 at age 52). She was 23 years old and 1.8km (1.1 miles) from the blast center when the bomb was dropped. She suffered aftereffects such as high fever, loss of hair, and erythema group (red macular spots on skin). Amid physical and psychological pain and financial difficulty, she felt depressed looking at the Peace Statue built at the immense cost of 30 million yen, and wrote this poem.

While delivering telegrams, I often dropped by Sumako's house to chat with her, so I was familiar with her difficult conditions. But she was not the only one. There were so many A-bomb survivors in dire straits because there were no governmental measures to support us. Calling for official measures to alleviate our suffering, Nihon Hidankyo started campaigning for state compensation for the A-bomb damage immediately after its founding in 1956.

With rising public voice calling for relief measures for the *hibakusha*, in April 1957, the Act for Atomic Bomb Sufferers' Medical Care (A-Bomb Medical Care Act) was adopted. At last, after 12 long years, *hibakusha* were entitled to health examinations and medical treatment relating to A-bomb induced diseases, with the costs covered by the government. I, too, was freed from worries about my medical bills. This was achieved by peoples' efforts and campaigns in the three years following the Bikini tragedy.

Unfortunately, the number of applications from *hibakusha* fell short of our expectations. Why? The compensation was so small. Free medical care was granted only to those whose illnesses were recognized as "A-bomb diseases" caused by the A-bomb radiation. Out of the 200,984 *hibakusha* who applied for and received the Atomic Bomb Sufferers Certificate in 1957, only 1,668 were acknowledged by the government as suffering from A-bomb diseases. The government set rigorous recognition criteria to distinguish A-bomb disease patients from general war victims. There were also many *hibakusha* who chose not to apply for fear of discrimination and prejudice.

Another serious shortcoming was that the law did not include measures to support *hibakushas'* costs of living. Due to poor health and illnesses caused by the atomic bombings, many *hibakusha* could not find work or stay employed. Many became quickly fatigued and could not perform their duties as well as others, a condition often called "A-bomb *bura bura* disease," which appeared to others as just being lazy. Such was the real life situation of many *hibakusha*.

The A-Bomb Medical Care Act was the first law established for us, but it was only the first step of our long struggle to improve relief measures for *hibakusha*.

Hibakushas' situation not understood

In 1957, the year the A-Bomb Medical Care Act took effect, the venue for the Third World Conference against A and H Bombs was set in Tokyo. Several members of our Association, including myself, travelled from Nagasaki to join the conference which was held at Yoyogi Gymnasium. The conference wasted little time in pointing out the shortcoming of the A-Bomb Medical Care Act and passed a resolution to continue the fight to urge the government to improve the law.

I had one unforgettable experience there. It happened at Kudan Kaikan Hall in Chiyoda-ku, the hotel assigned to the members of local delegations. While some of the Nagasaki *hibakusha* were chatting in the lobby, a male student and representative of another prefecture approached us and said, "It's already been ten years since the atomic bombing. You should stop whining."

I stood up and said to him, "We are not whining, but shedding tears of mortification. It makes me cry more when I think about those who have died." I felt so frustrated and tears kept filling my eyes. Suddenly, I found myself taking off my jacket, revealing the scars on my bare back to him and crying, "We are working hard so that no one should ever suffer such a fate. How can you not understand us?" The student looked embarrassed and left without a word.

With the World Conference being held for the third time, I had thought that the plight and difficulties of the *hibakusha* were understood more broadly and that the general public was beginning to treat us more warmly. But one step out of Nagasaki or Hiroshima, we found that the reality was totally different. There might be some people who were envious of us, thinking that the *hibakusha* were unduly given preferential treatment. It was all the more shocking for me since a conference participant had shown this type of attitude.

Long after that, Ms. Yamaguchi Miyoko, who was with me in the Nagasaki Hisaikyo delegation to the World Conference, told me, "At that time, I was so surprised to see you so furious." I did not mean to be like that; maybe I was just young then. But the student's remark must have really burned me up, as I used to hide my back and tried not to put my scars on display.

In September 1957, shortly after the World Conference that year, Nihon Hidankyo, in close cooperation with Gensuikyo, convened its national assembly in Hiroshima and began the work of collecting and preserving evidence of the *hibakushas'* situation, including their essays and other life records and photographs. It marked the beginning of the *hibakushas'* activities to make the damage and aftereffects of the atomic bombing known to people in Japan and all over the world.

In front of Suginami Public Hall, one of the workshop venues of the third World Conference against A and H Bombs

Trip to East Germany for medical treatment

The international community was already in the midst of an uncontrollable nuclear arms race when Nihon Hidankyo was formed in August 1956. In competition with the U.S., the Soviet Union successfully conducted its first nuclear test in 1949, and this was followed by Great Britain and France.

As stated in Hidankyo's founding declaration, in order to save humanity from the crisis of nuclear war, *hibakusha* began to join delegations to travel overseas for speaking tours. Mr. Yamaguchi Senji, who invited me to join the movement, was chosen to be on Gensuikyo's delegation in 1961. He assumed the important mission of testifying about his A-bomb experience, touring several European countries including Germany. By coincidence,

I travelled to Germany in April that same year.

A trade union from East Germany, a country with advanced medical technology, extended an invitation to the *hibakusha* to get medical treatment through the General Council of Trade Unions of Japan (Sohyo). In addition to myself, a *hibakusha* from Hiroshima was chosen. I had given up on the scars on my back and chest, but hoped something could be done to my left arm, which I could not stretch beyond 110 degrees.

It took more than 20 hours to fly from Haneda Airport in Tokyo to West Germany. From there we used a car to enter East Germany. As Germany was divided in two and placed at the forefront of the Cold War, I felt nervous and worried about crossing the border safely, but they let me through after seeing my passport.

After a detailed examination and one month in the hospital, I was told that they could not operate on my body due to my chronic hematopoietic (blood-producing function) disorder. That explained why I got tired so easily, but I was disappointed. At the same time, I was furious remembering the "No abnormality detected" result of my U.S. ABCC examination.

I was taken to a resort facility on a mountain and spent the remaining three months there. Many tourists visited the place, and I showed them pictures of Nagasaki taken immediately after the atomic bombing and shared my experience. It was my first experience telling my story to non-Japanese people.

Before leaving Japan, I promised Senji that we would get together in East Germany, but after all, he did not come. I thought maybe he could not cross the border due to heightened political confrontation, but later I learned that he had to cut his trip short and go back to Japan just before I entered East Germany. He was indeed suffering badly from the aftereffects of the atomic bombing.

In August 1961, immediately after I came back home, East Germany closed its borders with West Berlin and embarked on building the Berlin Wall.

CHAPTER 5

My Life Partner

First meeting with Eiko

"What an arrogant guy." "She is just another woman." These were the first impressions my wife Eiko (83 years old now) and I had of each other. We met each other for the first time on March 1, 1956. I was 27 and Eiko was 25. The World Conference against A and H Bombs in Nagasaki was approaching and our movement had been gaining momentum.

Here I would like to talk about my family. After my broken-hearted attempt to kill myself, Grandpa introduced me to some women for an arranged marriage. But because I was a *hibakusha*, I was rejected five or six times. I had a badly burned back, and I was not sure whether I would live for long, so I had given up the hope of getting married. My only concern was my grandmother Taga, who had been taking care of me after my mother passed away. She had been bedridden for about a year, and we were told that she didn't have much time left. She often said in her delirium, "Sumiteru is still single."

Begged by Grandma, my aunt found Eiko for me. Eiko was born in Korea. After the World War, she and her family came back to Togitsu, her father's hometown in Nagasaki. I met Eiko in the shop where she was working. It was in Hama-machi in Nagasaki City where Japanese buns filled with red bean paste were sold. I remember that we hardly talked that day. "Can I get some buns?" I said. I bought some and left for home.

Between her work and helping on the family farm, Eiko led a busy life at that time and didn't plan on getting married. Having been hurt by my previous experience, I also didn't feel like getting married. Maybe because my aunt pressured her, Eiko decided to accept me. And because I wanted Grandma to feel at ease, I also decided to get married.

We held our wedding ceremony at my house on the side of Mt. Inasayama ten days after we first met. I was glad that one of my colleagues at the telegraph office attended. Eiko looked nervous and was in a sullen mood the whole time. Anxiety was whirling through my mind, as I wondered, "How much has my aunt told Eiko about me?" After the ceremony, Eiko and I went to my grandmother who was in bed in the next room. In tears, Grandma held Eiko's hands and said, "I leave Sumiteru to you."

The next day we went to Unzen, a famous hot spring resort, for our honeymoon. One of my colleagues came to the bus station to see us. We were close friends, and I had told him all about myself and my worries. When our bus was about to leave, he rushed over to Eiko and said to her, "I'll be counting on you," and bowed. She looked at him with a puzzled expression on her face.

My anxiety during the honeymoon

The entire bus ride to Unzen, I hardly talked to Eiko because I was so worried about that night. She might leave me when she sees my back. Yes, she will leave me for sure. The idea came to my mind again and again, and I couldn't bring myself to hold a conversation with Eiko. She may have thought that I was angry.

It was already dark when we arrived at Midoriya Inn, which was run by a friend of mine. When we finished our dinner, I had made up my mind and said to her, "Let's have a bath together. Can you wash off my back?" In the bathroom, I sat on the stool with my back toward her. I could sense her gasping in shock. Still, without saying anything, she washed my back. I heard her sobbing quietly. Because of my fear, I couldn't look back.

She continued sobbing after we got into bed, and she still shed tears on and off the following day. She had been born in Korea and had spent her life there until the war ended. She didn't know what had happened in Hiroshima and Nagasaki. I started to talk about myself. Bit by bit, I told her about my mail delivery job during the war, what I experienced on August 9, 1945, and my long days in the hospital.

Long after that, when she was giving an interview to a newspaper reporter, I came to learn what was on her mind at that time. Before we married, my aunt had told Eiko that I only had minor burns on my face and arms. So when she saw my back so severely burned that first night of our honeymoon, her first thought was "I was cheated." But she said to the reporter, "I also was shocked, and learned how cruel the A-bomb was, and I could not stop crying." When she calmed down, she made up her mind to support and take care of me.

When we got home after our two days of honeymoon, we were surprised to be greeted by my relatives who had attended our wedding. I later learned that they had stayed at the house because they were too worried to leave my grandparents and go home. They thought that Eiko would not come back with me after seeing the wounds on my back.

I brought Eiko to my Grandma's bedside. She looked so happy when she saw we had returned together. She took Eiko's hands and said, "Thank you" in a shaking voice. She passed away ten days later, on March 23rd, 1956. She looked peaceful in death.

Joy of becoming a father

At the telegraph office, we were required to work early morning, evening, and night shifts. Eiko appeared a little uneasy because I needed to work irregular hours, but she supported me without any complaints. I was not able to sweat, as the sweat glands on my back had been damaged, and I didn't eat much because the skin on my back could tear if I gained weight. In order to stay in good condition, I abstained from drinking, also. She would joke to friends saying, "I'm lucky to have a husband who's so easy to care for. It doesn't take any trouble to prepare a meal for him or wash his clothes."

Around the end of October 1956, Eiko told me that she was pregnant. I felt a surge of joy, but soon fear took over. I was worried that my child might be born with health problems. Now it is said that the effects of radiation from the A-bomb will not be passed on to children, but there was no information available then. And there were many *hibakusha* around me whose children were disabled. Though we didn't discuss the matter, I believe Eiko was worried as well.

One month before the baby was due, Eiko was hospitalized. She had become ill and nearly miscarried. I blamed myself for being a *hibakusha* and wished only that I'd never been exposed to radiation. At that time, the husband was not supposed to attend his wife's delivery, so I spent my days just praying.

On that day in July 1957, I received word and rushed to the maternity hospital. I took my baby girl into my arms. She was a perfectly healthy and very beautiful girl. When I thought that such a healthy baby was born as my daughter, I felt myself letting go of tension with great relief. "You did a great job," I told Eiko. She smiled.

Taking the first letters from our names, we named the baby "Sumie." She grew up without any health problems. Because I had late evening and night shifts, I often was at home during the daytime and played with Sumie. Though I couldn't carry her on my back or give her horsey rides as a normal parent would, I often rocked her in my arms.

Two years after Sumie was born, Eiko became pregnant again, and again I worried whether this baby would be born healthy. But a boy came into the world without any problems. I named my long-awaited son "Hideo." Not so long before, I could not imagine that I would get married and have two children. "I'm so glad to have survived," I thought from the bottom of my heart.

Sumie and Hideo grew up without any serious diseases. Now they have their own families and I have four grandchildren and two great-grandchildren.

My Life Partner

Pregnant Eiko. Though we never talked about it, we worried about whether the baby would be born with any problems.

Supported by family

In 1960, one year after Hideo was born, I was suffering from pain in my back. Even after my discharge from the National Omura Hospital (formerly the Omura Naval Hospital) in the spring of 1949, the wound around my left shoulder had still not completely closed and a hard lump was about to be formed underneath the wound.

The inner lump gradually grew bigger and finally stuck out through the keloid scars on my back. It hurt when the lump touched my clothes, and I felt severe pain every time I lay on my back. I had the lump scraped several times in the hospital, and they were so hard that they nicked the scalpel blade. I asked Eiko to scrape it away with a razor at home, but it was too hard to do it. At last, I requested that my doctor remove them from the root.

I went to the Nagasaki A-Bomb Hospital in Katafuchi-machi (currently Mori-machi), Nagasaki City. The Japanese Red Cross Society opened the hospital in May 1958 to provide complete treatment and cures for the *hibakusha*. The Red Cross hospital for *hibakusha* in Hiroshima had been established two years before. The Nagasaki A-Bomb Youth and Maidens Association and Nagasaki Hisaikyo had petitioned for such a hospital to be built in Nagasaki in order to treat the large number of *hibakusha* suffering from the effects of the bomb.

On the day of the surgery, I was told that if things went wrong I would die because of the dysfunction in my ability to produce blood. I wasn't worried though, because the surgeon was the number one student of Professor Shirabe Raisuke of Nagasaki University, who had performed many surgeries on me. I underwent the operation without anxiety.

Using local anesthesia, the surgeon opened the scar with a scalpel and removed the lump below, which was shaped like a big scab three to four centimeters in diameter. The doctor told me to take it back home for memory, and I still keep it wrapped in cotton.

I was in the hospital for two weeks, and Eiko came to see me every day, taking Sumie by the hand and Hideo in her arms. "Are you all right? How do you feel?" she asked with concern. Now that I had a family, I felt secure and happy.

Even after that operation, lumps continue to grow out of my back. I have undergone 24 operations and the latest one was in the spring of 2012. I always request to my doctor that after I die, he should strip the entire skin from my back and use it for the study of and cure for *hibakusha*.

My Life Partner

Thanks to support from my family, I have been able to survive to this day.

A decision to visit a beach

My two children grew older without any problems. They vigorously ran about the same hillside where my older brother and I used to play around catching Japanese white-eyes. One of my joys was to give them baths when they were covered in mud from playing.

As Sumie grew, she began to worry about the keloid scarring on my back. Whenever we took a bath together, she asked me what had happened to my back. I answered, "You will see when you grow up." I didn't mean to dodge the question, but I thought that she was too young to understand things like the war and the atomic bombing.

Around that time, as we approached the summer, I became very upset because the children wanted to go to the beach. I feared that once my children noticed the difference between my back and other men's they would run away from me, so I didn't want to take them. But I thought it was impossible to continue to evade the question forever. After talking with Eiko, I made up my mind.

I suppose it was just before Sumie entered elementary school that I took my children to an amusement park in Ohamamachi, Nagasaki City. Today condominium buildings stand in the place where there used to be an amusement park called Fukuda no Yuenchi. The park included a go-cart facility, a Ferris wheel, and a beach. I changed into swim shorts and then put on a Hawaiian shirt Eiko had made for me. The shirt was to prevent my children from comparing my back with those of other fathers.

With this shirt on, I chased the children as we ran towards the sea. Another family played around us nearby. The children must have been aware of the difference between other men's backs and my own which they were used to seeing in the bath at home, but their demeanor didn't change at all. With some sense of relief, I took off my shirt in the sea.

After playing together for some time, the three of us came back to where Eiko was waiting. A towel was hanging around my neck but I no longer wore the shirt. If I remember correctly, I said to my children, "This was caused by the A-bomb." Neither Sumie nor Hideo asked any questions and I myself talked no more about that.

I have tried to let my children do and learn everything they wanted: study, sports, and other private lessons. I wasn't able to do as much as I desired because of the war and A-bombing. Sometimes this made me miserable. So I wanted my children not to suffer in this way.

My Life Partner

Living with my wife for half a century

After I get out of a bath, Eiko always puts some ointment on my back, using an antibiotic ointment on the sore places and then moisturizer. Without it, a back with no perspiration glands and sebum might crack like a dried-up rice paddy. This routine has continued for more than half a century, beginning the evening we returned from our honeymoon.

When I put on weight, thin skin on my back is strained and causes pain. Thus I am careful about my diet every day. Eiko makes meals with fish and miso soup, and I avoid meat and oil as much as possible.

Without complaining, Eiko supported me as I gradually became engaged in the *hibakusha* movement. I traveled around the country and even traveled overseas 23 times to talk about my experience. Eiko always stayed at home and waited for me. I am sure that at first she was unhappy, but from early on she has been very understanding.

In the mid-1970s, when major countries conducted nuclear testing as if in competition, *hibakusha* began a sit-in protest. The tests were carried out so often that I had to go out to the protest on each of my days off. Not only did Eiko not complain, she even took part in the protests together with the children.

As I started to play more visible roles in the *hibakusha* movement, I received more interviews from the media and some of them came from abroad. They visited our home and asked Eiko about every detail of our life, including the early years of our marriage. There must have been things she didn't want to talk about. I must have caused her so much hardship.

Although I am grateful to my wife, I sometimes make a slip of the tongue and crack a bad joke when I am with her. Recently, while putting old pictures in order, I found a family photo in the zoo. I pointed to a picture of a gorilla and said, "This is you." Looking at the photo, Eiko got angry and hit me over the head, saying, "This is an ape. I will kick you out."

When the pain on my back is so severe, I cannot help but to complain while Eiko puts ointment on my back. She always responds, "You should complain to the atomic bomb. Go to the United States, take off your clothes, and show your body." Whenever I am disheartened, she repeatedly encourages me like that. Only with her support have I been able to continue the struggle to this day.

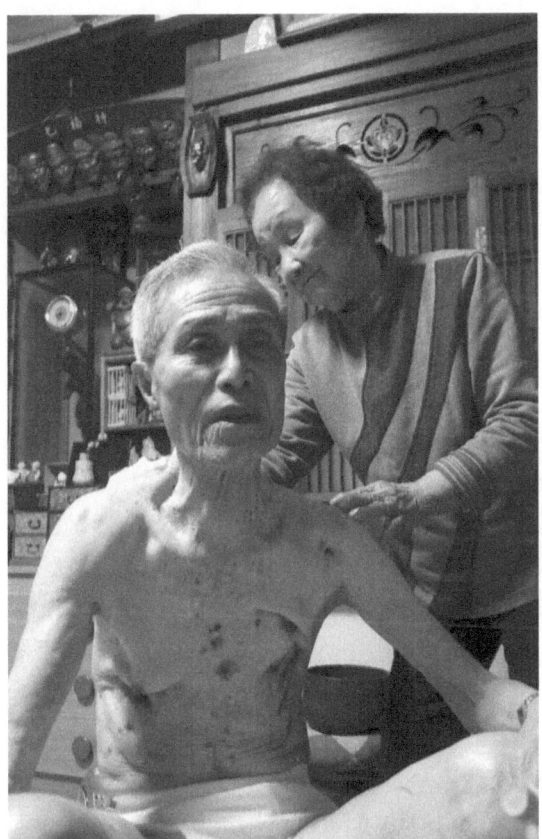

Eiko is rubbing cream over my back. This has been her everyday routine for over half a century.

Note: Eiko died on April 30, 2016 at age 86.

CHAPTER 6:

In the Midst of the Storm Splitting the Movement

Japan shaken by the Japan-U.S. Security Treaty

After having been ruled by the General Headquarters of the Allied Forces (GHQ) since the end of World War II, Japan recovered its sovereignty when the San Francisco Peace Treaty took effect in 1952. At this time it also entered into a mutual security treaty with the U.S. During the period from 1959 to 1960, nationwide confrontations over this treaty convulsed all of Japan.

It was triggered by a campaign by the Liberal Democratic Party (LDP) to amend the terms of the treaty, stating that it was not equal. The LDP was trying to modify this treaty which had simply endorsed the stationing of U.S. troops in Japan and surrounding areas into one which would make Japan responsible for the defense of the U.S. stationing troops. The opposition parties stood firm against the revision of the treaty, claiming that "it would drag Japan into war."

In those days, the world was at the height of the Cold War. Conflicts had broken out in many parts of the world. As it wasn't long since the Pacific War had ended, I seriously worried that the world might be returning war again. Trade unions opposed the security treaty with the U.S. and organized struggles against it in many cities. At the telegraph office in Omura City which was a base for the struggle, I joined with other workers to go on a 24-hour strike. The Nippon Telegraph and Telephone Public Corporation punished the employees who participated in strikes. The penalties were especially severe in the Nagasaki branch, and two workers were fired. I myself suffered a salary cut.

In May 1960, exasperated by the spread of the struggle against the treaty revision, the cabinet of Prime Minister Kishi Nobusuke ordered a police squad to storm the Committee of the House of Representatives (Lower House) to remove the politicians opposing the revision. Then Kishi rammed through the ratification of the revised Japan-U.S. Security Treaty at the plenary session of the Lower House. Thousands of citizens who witnessed this sensed a crisis of democracy and took to the streets in protest. In June, James Hagerty, an aide to U.S. President Dwight D. Eisenhower, came to Japan to prepare the ground for an official visit to Japan by the president. Hagerty's car was surrounded by tens of thousands of demonstrators, and he had to be rescued by the U.S. Marine Corps helicopter. Five days later riot police clashed with demonstrators in front of the Diet building. A woman student from the University of Tokyo who was participating in the demonstration died in that clash.

Gensuikyo, which led the anti-nuclear weapons movement, was also against the revision of the Security Treaty. The organization feared that Japan would be made a military base for nuclear wars initiated by the United States. Though I myself did not go, some members of the Nagasaki A-Bomb

Youth Association went to Tokyo to join the protest actions in response to Gensuikyo's call.

Later in June, the revised Japan-U.S. Security Treaty was automatically enacted without being voted on in the House of Councilors (Upper House). Amidst harsh popular criticisms, the Kishi Cabinet had to step down. The new cabinet led by Prime Minister Ikeda Hayato came to power proposing the so-called "Income-Doubling Plan." The turmoil subsided, but the struggle against the Japan-U.S. Security Treaty drove a wedge in the anti-nuclear weapons movement, which had enjoyed almost unanimous popular support. This led to a split in the movement which continues unsettled to this day.

A crack in the anti-A and H bomb movement

Triggered by the Lucky Dragon No. 5 Incident, the movement against A and H bombs gained momentum and developed nationwide. The movement remained united despite the differences in ideas and beliefs among the Japanese citizens who were involved. But it took a negative turn when arguments began inside the movement over the revision of the Japan-U.S. Security Treaty. The movement gradually grew political, leaving A-bomb survivors out of the loop.

In March 1959, Gensuikyo, the key player in the movement, formed the National Council for the Prevention of the Revision of the Japan-U.S. Security Treaty (National Council) with the Japan Socialist Party (JSP) and the General Council of Trade Unions of Japan (Sohyo) in order to conduct a full-fledged struggle against the treaty's revision. In response, the ruling Liberal Democratic Party took a hostile position towards Gensuikyo. In July it ordered local governments to stop providing financial assistance to the local branches of Gensuikyo. A major goal was to drive conservative local council members away from the movement which had to that point involved local councils, progressive and conservative alike.

In this context, ideology took center stage during the sixth World Conference against A and H Bombs. The final resolution referred to not only "the abrogation of Security Treaty," but also to "U.S. Imperialism." Reacting to this move, the Democratic Socialist Party seceded from Gensuikyo the following year and founded the National Council for Peace and against Nuclear Weapons (Kakkin-Kaigi).

The Japan Socialist Party (JSP) and the Japanese Communist Party (JCP), which had been struggling jointly against the Japan-U.S. Security Treaty, became deeply divided over the renewal of nuclear tests by the Soviet Union in 1961. The JSP was "against nuclear tests by any country," while the JCP claimed that it was wrong to discuss nuclear tests conducted by a socialist country for defense against those conducted by an imperialist country. Because of the conflict between these two influential groups within Gensuikyo, the anti-A and H bombs movement fell into serious disarray.

Two years later, the sparks of conflict smoldering inside Gensuikyo flared up again when the United States, the United Kingdom, and the Soviet Union signed the Partial Nuclear Test Ban Treaty (PTBT). While the JSP supporters favored the treaty, the JCP supporters opposed it because "the treaty would endorse underground nuclear testing."

It was the Cold War, and it was understandable to claim that the nuclear tests by the Soviet Union had only defense purposes. It was also acceptable to argue that the PTBT was fruit of the movement. But our goal was a total ban on atomic and hydrogen bombs. I tried to persuade the two groups that they should talk to each other with patience, but they would not listen to me, insisting that they would not be able to collaborate with people they disagreed with.

In August 1963, the JSP group boycotted the World Conference and held their own meeting. Eventually the conference split.

In a storm of the movement's split

In 1963, the World Conference, having been a symbol of the united movement against A and H bombs, split up. There should have been unanimous support for the ultimate goal of abolishing all nuclear weapons, but the movement was disrupted because some activists put their party interests first, sticking to their respective principles.

In April 1964, while efforts to re-unite the movement continued, six organizations, including the JSP and Sohyo, held a national meeting of representatives of anti-A and H bomb movements in Hiroshima, where they decided to hold another world conference separately from Gensuikyo. We, the members of the Nagasaki A-Bomb Youth and Maidens Association, were distressed to learn the news from newspaper reports. We were afraid that the movement would be stagnant if it remained divided.

We immediately had a meeting with other A-bomb survivors' organizations and at a press conference issued an open letter asking for the explanation about why they had to split the World Conference. The Japan Socialist Party criticized us in its party newspaper saying, "The open letter is faked. It was produced by a bogus group of merely two or three A-bomb survivors."

We were outraged by this remark. Ms. Fukuda Sumako, a poet, became so angry that she insisted on storming into the JSP building. I desperately tried to persuade her not to do that, saying, "They are anything but reasonable. Don't be emotional and add fuel to the fire, or it will make things worse."

We had a strong attachment to Gensuikyo because we were proud that we ourselves had helped build it to what it had become. At the very beginning of the movement against A and H bombs, Gensuikyo held consultation meetings with A-bomb survivors around the country so that the movement would become a "genuine movement." Whenever it was asked by Gensuikyo, the Nagasaki Council of A-Bomb Survivors sent members from the Nagasaki A-Bomb Youth and Maidens Association to such meetings. As people stayed up late into the night talking about their experiences, local organizations of Gensuikyo were formed one after another. That was why the turmoil within Gensuikyo was terribly painful to me.

However, despite our efforts, the split became definite in 1965 when the JSP and Sohyo formed a separate organization named Gensuikin (the Japan Congress against A and H Bombs). Gensuikyo and Gensuikin held their world conferences separately and slandered each other. I was labeled as "red" or "Communist" because I participated in the conference held by Gensuikyo. Many A-bomb survivors, tired of such a chaotic situation, left the movement. Citizens' groups that had lent their support also withdrew from Gensuikyo. The movement that had once mobilized the entire nation against the Bomb thus rapidly lost momentum.

Today, Gensuikyo, Gensuikin, and Kakkin-Kaigi which was founded in 1961, still hold their conferences separately. I cannot help but feel frustrated thinking that if they had avoided the split by putting aside their differences, such as whether to oppose "nuclear tests by any country," the movement against nuclear weapons would have made more progress.

In the early days of Gensuikyo's founding, we were often invited to join meetings across the country to share our A-bomb experiences.
On my right is Mr. Yoshida Katsuji.

Hidankyo becomes dysfunctional

The split in the anti-nuclear weapons movement did more than driving A-bomb survivors away from the movement. It also forced those who were involved to choose to their affiliation from between three groups. The Japan Confederation of A-and H-Bomb Sufferers' Organizations (Hidankyo), which was affiliated with Gensuikyo before its split, went through serious internal conflicts.

At the regular general assembly of Hidankyo in 1962, eleven prefectural branches made a joint proposal to leave Gensuikyo or to affiliate with Kakkin-Kaigi at the same time. The long and heated deliberations that followed were inconclusive. In 1965, the same year that Gensuikin was founded, Hidankyo's board of representatives finally decided that Hidankyo would "not affiliate itself with any anti-nuclear weapons organization" and thus seceded from Gensuikyo.

Hidankyo's internal problem seemed settled for a while, but in fact the board did not meet for a whole year because of the rift created in the crisis. The previous year, both the House of Representatives and the House of Councilors passed a resolution strengthening official support for A-bomb survivors. That offered us a good opportunity to develop the movement, but by that point Hidankyo was simply too dysfunctional.

Many prefectural branches were also forced to split or were thrown into serious turmoil. On the issue of the Soviet nuclear tests, Hiroshima Prefectural Gensuikyo was divided due to disagreement about whether or not to oppose nuclear testing by all countries. Even today there are two Hidankyo organizations in Hiroshima Prefecture.

Nagasaki Hisaikyo (Nagasaki Council of A-Bomb Survivors) was able to avoid a split. I think we owe a great deal to Mr. Kosasa Hachiro's contributions as President.

Mr. Kosasa was one of the founders of Nagasaki Hisaikyo. He was familiar to all and nicknamed "Hacchan." Even when the arguments became very heated over the policies of the movement, he was able to calm the room with his open-hearted nature. On the other hand, he was the last person to give in to anything that ran contrary to his principles. He used to say, "We should avoid the split at any cost." I wonder where we would be without him.

At the same time, I must admit that some members did choose to leave us. These were the members of the Association of A-Bomb Victims of Mobilized Students. I learned this while I was attending a Gensuikyo meeting held in Oita, and I rushed back to Nagasaki to meet Mr. Fukahori Katsuichi, then the President of the association. I tried to convince him that he and I had made a promise to work together for our goal, but my arguments were in vain. His association was reorganized and is now part of the Nagasaki Association of A-Bomb Victims' Handbook Holders.

The split in the anti-nuclear weapons movement left grudges among A-bomb survivors. Looking at what was happening around the world then, especially as the Vietnam War raged increasing the risk of an atomic bomb being used again, I felt both frustrated and ashamed that the anti-nuclear weapons movement could not be united in facing these challenges.

Hibakusha and Vietnam

I was not able to avert my eyes from the photos in the newspaper, which showed innumerable slaughtered bodies of Vietnamese people floating in the waves of the Mekong River, or the children burnt seriously by the bombings. I identified these people with A-bomb victims, including myself. The war in Vietnam started in 1960, and day after day the media reported on the terrible battles and human suffering there. I saw myself in these tragedies that the people of Vietnam were enduring.

The Vietnam War was said to be a proxy war between the

United States and the Soviet Union. The threat of nuclear war receded following the Cuban Missile Crisis in 1962, but the United States continued its attacks in Vietnam using new types of weapons such as napalm, pineapple bombs, and Agent Orange. As the war was dragged on, we felt that atomic bombs could be used any time.

What was particularly unacceptable to us was that Japan was taking part in this war. Okinawa, ruled like a colony by the United States in those days, and other U.S. military bases around Japan were used as launching points to carry out attacks on Vietnam. In January 1968, the USS Enterprise, a nuclear-powered aircraft carrier, arrived at Sasebo Port. It appeared that Sasebo would become the key base for attacking North Vietnam.

People from progressive parties, students' groups, and trade unions from around the country gathered, marched, and staged mass demonstrations. I could not participate in the demonstration in Sasebo because I underwent surgery in my back on the same day. However I was with the demonstrators in spirit, and I watched on TV the clash between the marchers and the police.

In the meantime, the warfare spread and the anti-war feelings grew more and more intense in Japan and abroad. In 1963, a Vietnamese Buddhist monk burnt himself to death in protest against the war in front of the U.S. Embassy in Saigon (Ho Chi Minh City). This was the first anti-war suicide in Vietnam, and a number of peace activists followed in the United States. Every time I heard such sad news, I seriously considered that I should make a raid into the Diet building with bombs strapped around me.

I thought that by conducting a suicide protest I might change the situation: the Japanese government's assistance in the U.S. war, the anti-nuclear movement's ongoing division and inability to unite, and the lack of progress providing relief measures to A-bomb survivors. However, I soon changed my mind when I saw that those activists who killed themselves in protest against the war were all easily forgotten by the public. After all, I had to admit that the best I could do was to continue the movement with perseverance and patience.

In 1975, the Vietnam War ended with the U.S. essentially defeated. The protracted war had escalated, but no atomic bombs were used after all. I thought that this was because the A-bomb survivors had continued to talk about the tragedies in Nagasaki and Hiroshima. While the anti-A and H bomb movement was somewhat paralyzed, this fact encouraged and gave hope to A-bomb survivors.

Aiming to unite the movement

When the Vietnam War ended, a move began to reunite the divided movement. In May 1977, the top leaders of Gensuikyo and Gensuikin, who had been at loggerheads with each other, suddenly agreed to hold a united World Conference in Hiroshima. This may have been in anticipation of the NGO International Symposium on the Damage and Aftereffects of the Atomic Bombing of Hiroshima and Nagasaki, which was scheduled to be held soon after the decision.

The Symposium was to be held in Nagasaki and Hiroshima. The petitions to the United Nations made by Gensuikyo and Hidankyo since 1976 had resulted in the convening of this gathering which was to be devoted to the scientific study of the realities of A-bomb damage and the dissemination of these results to the rest of the world.

In preparation for the Symposium, organizations of A-bomb survivors and doctors met around the country to conduct a basic survey. About 8,000 A-bomb survivors participated by responding to a questionnaire. In the symposium held from the end of July to early August 1977, it became evident that the United Nations had underestimated the death toll in A-bombed Nagasaki and Hiroshima. The combined damage caused by the atomic blasts, heat rays, and radiation was made known for the first time in the international community.

Many groups and individuals joined the effort to hold this successful symposium. To capitalize on that initiative, many A-bomb survivors, including myself and citizens groups, called for the reunification of the anti-nuclear weapons movement. I think Gensuikyo and Gensuikin agreed to re-unite because both feared to lose people's support if they could not agree to work together.

The unified conference was held in Hiroshima for the first time in 14 years. I heard it was an unbelievably peaceful gathering. A-bomb survivors and citizens who had been absent from the movement for a long time returned. The stadium, which had a capacity of 9,000, was packed with conference delegates. I was really glad to hear that.

Unfortunately, however, the conference split again in 1986. The dispute about opposing nuclear tests by any country had been already settled, but skirmishes still took place between Gensuikyo and Gensuikin. I think this was caused by the enduring emotional confrontations rather than political differences. The split was very painful for us because we had so longed for the reunification. "What should we believe in to continue the movement?" I shouted with rage against one of the board members of Gensuikyo who came to Nagasaki.

Some people say there should be many roads leading to the elimination of nuclear weapons, but I do not think so. As long as the movement remains divided, the problem will be politicized, and the movement will not spread throughout the whole nation. A-bomb survivors do not have much time left. Whatever the reasons that have divided people or put them against each other in the past, I hope that they will overcome them and unite for the common goal of eliminating all nuclear weapons.

CHAPTER 7

'Reddened Back' Shown to the Public

My reddened back shown to the public

"Will you please check a photo in the newspaper for us? We will bring you a copy shortly." I will never forget receiving this telephone call on the morning of June 21, 1970 from the Tokyo office of the Asahi Shimbun. It was Sunday, and I wondered what was going on. I was surprised to see an article in the paper the reporter brought to me with a photo of a boy lying on his face, his back reddened, grimacing in pain. Undoubtedly, the boy was me.

Although I did not remember this picture being taken, I vividly recalled the hellish agony and the smell of rotten flesh peeling off from my chest. When my wife saw the picture, she muttered, "How remarkable it is that you survived…"

I learned from the reporter that the picture had been taken from a 16mm color movie film discovered at the U.S. National Archives in Washington, D.C. The film was taken very soon after the bombing by U.S. forces. The newspaper also featured photos of keloid scars on a *hibakusha*'s hand, the Atomic Bomb

"Reddened Back" Shown to the Public

Dome in Hiroshima, and Urakami Cathedral, which the Nagasaki A-bomb destroyed in an instant.

A week after the paper was printed, the Nagasaki Broadcasting Company and six other commercial broadcasting stations around the country aired the film footage at 8 a.m. I watched it in the Nagasaki Telegraph Office along with my colleagues after working an overnight shift.

The footage showed a bony blood-stained back moving up and down with each breath the boy took. When a nurse applied a piece of gauze soaked in a liquid medicine on his back, the boy's face looked pained. As I remembered, I murmured, "This was Omura Naval Hospital." On January 31, 1946, a U.S. soldier came to film me. I was screaming day after day, "Kill me, please."

As I watched the video, I noticed that my hair had fallen off. Loss of hair is one of the acute symptoms that emerge after exposure to radiation. But there was no way I would have been worrying about my hair, since I could not move even an inch. In 1947, when I saw my back for the first time on my own, I saw my hair growing back.

Until then, the footage of the A-bomb damage that had been made public was in black and white. The release of the color film provided many people with much more vivid images of *hibakusha* and the bombed areas. The broadcasting station received so many inquiries that they aired the film the following day as well.

The photo of my reddened back and the released color film not only informed the public of the terrors of the A-bomb; it also changed my 41-year-old life in a drastic way.

The Atomic Bomb On My Back

An image showing my red back was also carried in the photo magazine *Asahi Graph* and changed my life.

Pushed onto center stage

I began to hear people talk a lot about the picture soon after it became widely known to the public. "Taniguchi Sumiteru with the reddened back" leapt into fame among people and places that I did not know.

I had been involved with the movement against A and H bombs since it began, but I had few opportunities to tell my A-bomb experience except when I was asked to do so in the workplace. In those days, Yamaguchi Senji, who had toured Europe speaking to different audiences, and Watanabe Chieko, who had been outspoken in calling for opposition to nuclear weapons from her wheelchair, were the main figures of the *hibakusha* movement. I supported the movement from behind the scenes, since I hated to display the scars on my back or hollows on my chest.

95

"Reddened Back" Shown to the Public

Today, it is very common for *hibakusha* to recount their A-bomb experience to students visiting Nagasaki on school trips, but this only began in the 1980s. In 1970, when the photo went public, the movement among *hibakusha* to record their A-bomb experiences grew, and collections of written testimonies were published one after another. I first wrote about my A-bomb experience when I prepared my contribution for Volume 2 of the Nagasaki Council of Atomic Bomb Survivors' collection. Many people, including those whom I had long been campaigning with, knew little about what I experienced. I remember many people saying, "I did not know you were so seriously injured."

I received many letters from around the country after *Asahi Graph*, a picture magazine, carried a photo of my back on two facing pages in July, 1970. Most were sympathetic to me, saying, "You must have undergone unbearable pains."

One thing came to my mind as I read the letters: "The suffering caused by the atomic bomb cannot be explained by the pain we experienced. The real question I want to raise with you is who is responsible for this terrible suffering."

As I began to talk to one journalist after another, I tried to explain in detail about my experience because I knew that photos alone could not convey the real damage of the atomic bombing. A British TV crew came to see me in Nagasaki. I had no idea how they came to know about me, but for the first time I took off my shirt in front of a camera to show the vivid scars on my back.

After this, I had more opportunities to give speeches at meetings and rallies. Unlike Yamaguchi Senji or Watanabe Chieko, I did not volunteer to speak in public. When I was first asked to take center stage, I took the microphone reluctantly.

I felt uncomfortable speaking before an audience, and I had difficulty projecting my voice due to my injuries. But I came to realize that now that a photo of my injury was publicly viewable, I could not refuse. I gradually made up my mind to be at the forefront.

"Pledge for peace"

In 1955, Kitamura Seibo, a sculptor from Nagasaki, produced a peace statue standing in Nagasaki with its right hand pointing upward to the threat of atomic bombs, its left hand extending outward towards peace, and its eyes somewhat closed in a prayer dedicated to the atomic bomb victims.

As part of an effort to attract tourists, Nagasaki City began removing the remnants of the atomic bombing in areas close to the hypocenter of the atomic bomb explosion. The fancy statue that stands in the middle of the cleaned-up area looked as if to say, "Get rid of everything that is detestable." *Hibakusha* were angered by the fact that at the same time no public support was given to them, 30 million yen was spent on building the statue. I feel sorry for Kitamura but I must say that I have stood with the *hibakusha* regarding the statue.

Every summer, people assemble in front of this statue to attend the peace memorial ceremony. I attended it for the first time in 1974, when the municipal government asked me to read a "Pledge for Peace" on behalf of the *hibakusha*. At first I thought I should decline the invitation because I did not believe an annual event like this could represent the heart of the *hibakusha* or be anything more than a formality.

Nevertheless I accepted the invitation. With nuclear powers conducting nuclear tests, and India joining the nuclear club in

May of that year, nuclear proliferation was a serious problem. The Japanese government was half-hearted in dealing with these developments and had no intention of legislating the Three Non-Nuclear Principles (not to possess or produce nuclear weapons, or allow them to enter Japan). There were even rumors that Japan was preparing to develop nuclear weapons. I felt I had to confront these adverse developments for the A-bomb victims who had died without knowing anything about them. Fortunately, I had the freedom to draft my speech as I liked.

I let out my anger during the hushed ceremony on a sweltering day that was just like the day when the A-bomb was dropped. "I pledge in front of the A-bomb victims that we will spare no effort to warn the world about the threat of nuclear weapons and force the Japanese government to take initiative at the United Nations to achieve an agreement to ban nuclear weapons."

To my regret, nothing has changed in the attitude of the Japanese government since I gave that speech. In the spring of 2013, South Africa and other countries proposed the "Joint Statement on the Humanitarian Consequences of Nuclear Weapons" at the Preparatory Committee for the Review Conference of the Parties to the Treaty on the Non-Proliferation of Nuclear Weapons. More than 70 countries supported the Joint Statement, but Japan did not. Apparently, Japan wanted to avoid an adverse impact on the "nuclear umbrella" provided by the United States. Shouldn't Japan, as the only country that has suffered A-bomb attacks, take the lead for the abolition of nuclear weapons? I cannot repress my indignation at the actions of my government.

Note: The government of Japan changed its policy in the face of criticism from the A-bombed cities. In October 2013 it joined the "Joint Statement on the Humanitarian Consequences of Nuclear Weapons" announced at the UN General Assembly First Committee by New Zealand and other countries. The statement made clear that "It is in the interest of the very survival of humanity that nuclear weapons are never used again, under any circumstances," but it did not mention "the outlawing of nuclear weapons" which had been included in previous statements. It is safe to say that the Japanese government's position of relying on the nuclear deterrence provided by the United States has not changed. The Joint Statement was supported by 125 countries or two-thirds of the United Nations member states. The nuclear powers, including the United States and China, did not support it.

Nuclear-powered ship, 'Mutsu'

On April 30, 1977, during the last day of an extraordinary session, the Nagasaki Prefectural Assembly convened to decide whether to allow the nuclear-powered ship *Mutsu* to enter Sasebo Port. Assembly chairman Matsuda Kuro ordered the heckling protestors to be forced out of the gallery by police officers, who pulled them out of their seats. Only 20 *hibakusha* remained seated in the gallery. I felt so frustrated that the assembly session was ignoring dissenting opinions that I shouted out loud, "Don't you know what the *hibakusha* are feeling?"

In the 1960s, Japan pursued nuclear power to meet the country's growing needs for electricity amid high economic growth, and in 1966 began operating its first commercial reactor. The nuclear-powered *Mutsu* was built as a symbol to promote nuclear power generation.

But the *Mutsu* leaked radiation on September 1, 1974 while it was on an experimental voyage. The residents of Mutsu City in Aomori, where the ship had its homeport, rejected the ship's return to the port due to the accident. The vessel was left to drift at sea. Sasebo in Nagasaki Prefecture emerged as a candidate port to accept the ship for repair. I heard that Mayor Tsuji Ichizo of Sasebo City offered to allow the ship to use the port hoping that it would help the financially struggling Sasebo Heavy Industries Company.

Nagasaki is an A-bombed prefecture, and its main industry is fisheries. How could we agree to receive the *Mutsu*? *Hibakusha* organizations, the fisheries cooperative union, and labor unions opposed the idea. At issue was whether the ship would enter the port with or without the nuclear fuel. While Sasebo City said it would accept the ship with the nuclear fuel, Nagasaki Prefecture Governor Kubo Kanichi insisted on entry without the nuclear fuel. We opposed entry even without the nuclear fuel, because we believed there would be no way to remove the nuclear fuel since the ship did not even have a homeport.

The governor proposed to "accept the ship to Sasebo Port for repair and maintenance on condition that she would enter the port without nuclear fuel." The prefectural assembly approved the proposal by majority. Tears came and I could not stop them. I thought the vote was an act of utter disrespect against the A-bomb survivors and those who were killed in the atomic bomb attack. My friends were all in tears.

In October 1978, the *Mutsu* entered Sasebo port with nuclear fuel. Just as we feared, they did not remove the nuclear fuel because they were unable to solve the problems of homeport and cost. They tried to legitimize this failure by stating that they had "sealed the nuclear fuel," meaning that they suspended the operation of the nuclear reactor. But there were rumors that in a political deal between the Nagasaki governor and top Liberal Democratic Party officials, the *Mutsu* was allowed to enter Sasebo in exchange for the construction of the Nagasaki route of the bullet train.

The national government is doing everything to promote nuclear power generation, using the deceptive argument that "nuclear energy is used for peaceful purposes." Safety concerns and public opinion are ignored, while local governments try to maintain a cozy relationship with the nuclear industry leaders. This attitude by the government eventually led to the nuclear accident at the Fukushima Daiichi plant.

Continuing protests against nuclear tests

397. Do you know what this number represents? It is the number of sit-ins we carried out in the last 40 years to protest nuclear tests. Often we were protesting nuclear testing that was taking place in more than one country at a time. The number of actual nuclear tests, however, is even higher than this.

We held our first sit-in on August 17, 1974. At the sit-in, five *hibakusha* teachers protested tests conducted by the U.S., the U.S.S.R., and France. One of the protesters, Yamakawa Takeshi, 76, explains, "We had been so infuriated by France and China's repeated atmospheric nuclear tests that we took action on that day."

After the Cuban Missile Crisis and other incidents, the United States, Britain, and the Soviet Union negotiated the Partial Test Ban Treaty in 1963, banning atmospheric nuclear tests. But two nuclear countries, France and China, did not sign the treaty. Radioactive fallout from their tests continued to fall all over the world. Meanwhile, the U.S., Britain, and the Soviet Union repeated underground tests, which were not banned by the treaty.

Members of the Nagasaki Hisaikyo joined soon Yamakawa's group. I joined the sit-in as a matter of course, since I was the chairman of the Nagasaki A-Bomb Youth and Maidens Association and often visited Hisaikyo office. At first, the sit-ins were held on the day that the news of a test was reported, but later we began to hold the gatherings on the Sunday following the test so more people could participate.

In July 1980, on the day of the 117th sit-in, we launched the "Nagasaki Citizens Association against Nuclear Tests." I was asked by other members to be the chair. Why me? Yamakawa said I was "the face of the *hibakusha* movement." It had been ten years since the photo of my reddened back was published, and I had come to be acknowledged by the people around me as a figure like Yamaguchi Senji and Watanabe Chieko.

Since then, the number of nuclear test explosions has sharply dropped. But nuclear powers, including the United States still conduct subcritical tests and test the performance of new types of nuclear weapons. The Japanese government does not protest such nuclear tests on the grounds that "tests that do not produce nuclear explosions do not violate the Comprehensive Test Ban Treaty." However, these tests are used to ensure the performance of nuclear weapons so that they can be used at any time. How intolerable it is for the government of the country that suffered the damage of the atomic bombing to take such a stance!

We will soon commemorate our 400th sit-in protest against nuclear tests. I agree with what Yamakawa once said: "We put our 'sane' argument, that nuclear weapons cannot co-exist with humanity, against the 'insane' position of nuclear powers, claiming that they can defend people with nuclear weapons. This is an endurance game between the two sides."

Note: The numbers of sit-ins are as of September 2013.

I attended a sit-in with Eiko to protest against nuclear tests.

CHAPTER 8:

Appealing to the World to Face the Reality of the A-Bombing

Attending international conference

After the picture of my "reddened back" became public, I had more opportunities to go abroad to talk about my atomic bomb experience. My overseas travel began in 1978. The first destination was Geneva, Switzerland, where I attended an international NGO conference on disarmament.

Two years earlier in 1978 the United Nations decided to hold the First Special Session of the UN General Assembly devoted to Disarmament (SSD-I) to pave the way for putting an end to a spate of nuclear tests and the unending arms race. The aim of the NGO conference was to help revitalize the anti-nuclear movement in preparation for the SSD-I. Fifteen people from Japan attended the conference, including members of Hidankyo, to make sure that A-bomb victims' voices were heard. I took part in the delegation.

Watanabe Chieko was among the group. She was rendered paraplegic by the injuries she suffered in the atomic bombing. She was in a wheelchair and that was her first trip abroad. I had not traveled out of Japan since my trip to East Germany for medical treatment. I pushed Chieko in her wheelchair as she eagerly looked around a shopping center during a stopover at an airport in Thailand.

Our cheap flight took us to our destination via Israel and France. It was amusing for us to see a group of elderly people traveling in the same flight. In *happi coats* bearing the rising sun of Japan's flag, they were very festive saying, "We're going to see the birthplace of Jesus Christ." Travelling by air was something special for many of us in those days. One of old men, complaining that he could not sleep, spread newspapers in the aisle and lay down on them. Another clogged the toilet. Chieko and I smiled wryly as we watched them.

On March 2, 1978, Chieko took the stage at the opening plenary of the International NGO Conference on Disarmament, which was attended by 511 people from 46 countries. She said, "The elimination of nuclear weapons should be possible even tomorrow, but only if the heart of the Japanese *hibakusha* is truly understood, and if the damage and aftereffects of the atomic bombings is well-known." Her powerful appeal helped turn the conference discussions toward building the force to pave the way for eliminating nuclear weapons. Philip Noel-Baker, a British anti-nuclear activist and Nobel Peace Prize laureate, hugged her gently. She was almost moved to tears.

Chieko used to say, "Were it not for the movement against A and H bombs, I would not have survived. The movement brought me back to life again." The same was true for me. Indeed, there were times when I cursed being *hibakusha*. But it is also true that we discovered the meaning of life by shouldering the task of abolishing nuclear weapons as our shared mission.

Appealing to the World to Face the Reality of the A-Bombing

Watanabe Chieko traveled overseas many times in her wheelchair to appeal against nuclear weapons and for peace.

Reactions from abroad

We held a Hiroshima-Nagasaki A-bomb photo exhibition and collected signatures in support of the abolition of nuclear weapons near the NGO International Conference on Disarmament in Geneva. Although we were not allowed to hold the photo panel exhibition in the UN office, we did manage to visit and petition officials from the nuclear powers.

After a week's stay in Geneva, the Japanese delegation was divided into six groups to visit different European countries to advocate for a nuclear weapon-free world. Chieko and I traveled to the Socialist Republic of Romania, which was under the influence of the Soviet Union. We faced problems from the outset.

When our plane arrived in Romania, Chieko's wheelchair was missing. We inquired about it at different offices but we were told that it would not reach us soon. Tentatively, we borrowed a wheelchair from a hospital, but it was very rickety and very difficult for Chieko, as her own wheelchair was specially made to fit to her body. She had to stay in her hotel room except to fulfill her speaking engagements at large meetings. Her wheelchair did not arrive until our departure from Romania. It came with its brakes broken.

I toured several places in Romania during my weeklong stay. Visiting schools and community centers, I spoke before many different people about what I had experienced as a *hibakusha*. Audiences ranged from elementary school children and secondary school students to adults, including academics and intellectuals. I called on them to work together to eliminate nuclear weapons, but my appeal drew only lukewarm reactions. The young audiences looked vacant, apparently unable to imagine the damage of the atomic bombings.

They said, "Romania does not have nuclear weapons, and we don't have to worry about being involved in nuclear war. We will be protected by the Soviet Union with nuclear weapons

Appealing to the World to Face the Reality of the A-Bombing

in an emergency." I found them completely lacking any sense of the crisis and the danger of nuclear war despite the escalating arms race. I was persistent, trying to let them know the danger of nuclear weapons by saying, "Anyone could be a victim of nuclear war as long as nuclear weapons exist." I also emphasized that "nuclear weapons are weapons of annihilation."

Three months after our European tour, the United Nations held the SSD-I at its headquarters in New York City. Romania did not send a delegate there, but the country was present in the SSD-II that was held four years later. I was so pleased to hear from Romanian activists that the *hibakushas'* appeal helped them to develop their movement for nuclear disarmament.

After the NGO International Conference on Disarmament, I traveled abroad many times to appeal for the abolition of nuclear weapons.

Give back the humans

The NGO International Conference on Disarmament and the SSD-I helped the global peace movement build momentum. Massive actions against nuclear weapons took place across in Europe and the United States.

Under these circumstances, Hidankyo received many requests from Europeans to send *hibakusha*. I traveled to Europe many times to talk about my experience.

I remember clearly what I experienced in Greece, where I had the opportunity to meet the deputy mayor of a city. When I showed him the scars in my back, he hugged me sobbing. I was surprised to see an adult man like him with tears on his cheeks expressing sympathy with me. I think this was because in the 1980s there was a sense of crisis over the danger of the outbreak of a nuclear war, because the U.S. and the Soviet Union had begun deploying intermediate-range missiles in Europe.

I also had another unexpected experience in Greece when I was kicked out of a souvenir shop. I was mistaken for a Communist because I was wearing the red crane button, one of the four colors, of Hidankyo. This demonstrated to me that we were indeed in the middle of the Cold War.

The "Ten Feet Movement" launched at the time was an important domestic initiative that we will never forget. This citizens' movement sought to collect donations to buy color films showing the devastated cities of Nagasaki and Hiroshima. The films were shot right after the bombings and stored in the U.S. National Archives. Each donor's contribution was used to pay for 10 feet of the films, which inspired the name of the movement.

The film footage shows Hibakusha with fresh scars and

keloids, including an image of me showing the reddened back. Film director Tachibana Yuten's group used these films to produce a three-part documentary film. In addition to myself, Ms. Kataoka Tsuyo, who suffered burns on her face when she was exposed to atomic bomb radiation, and Mr. Yamaguchi Senji are featured in the documentary. The film, "*Ningen wo kaese*" ("Give Us Back Our Humans") is shown today at the Nagasaki Atomic Bomb Museum. It contains scenes that may trigger you to close your eyes, but I do hope that you will watch the film.

Tachibana and his colleagues toured Europe showing the film. "The footage of Hiroshima and Nagasaki should not be treated as something of the distant past. In an era of the frantic arms race we see today, it projects what might be the future of you and our good earth." That's part of the narrative script read by actress Otake Shinobu. I hope that these words were taken by the people of Europe as a warning of imminent threats.

At this same time, the Second Special Session of the UN General Assembly devoted to Disarmament (SSD-II) was held in 1982. On that occasion we experienced an upsurge that I had never seen before in the movement against nuclear weapons.

A sense of exaltation I had never felt

The main streets of Manhattan were filled with people in June 1982 when the SSD-II opened in New York. One million people from around the world marched in a demonstration carrying banners reading "Abolish Nuclear Weapons."

My participation in the SSD-II was decided on very short notice at the request of the Nagasaki Prefectural Council of Trade Unions just a month before the special session was to begin. At that time, I was on a speaking tour in West Germany, having been sent by Hidankyo.

The labor council was a member of Gensuikin which had broken away from Gensuikyo. Although I sympathized with Gensuikyo, I willingly accepted the request to participate in the SSD-II because I thought I should be able to work with both groups in order to fulfill the *hibakushas'* mission.

Hidankyo was organizing a 41-member delegation to the SSD-II. Other peace organizations and citizens' groups also planned to send their members to New York. The total number of Japanese participants would have been 1,400, but over 200 people, mostly from Gensuikyo, were denied their visas. That was clearly an act of obstruction by the U.S. government. This infuriated me because the U.S. should have no right to obstruct entry into the country for people visiting the United Nations.

We arrived in New York to find the streets full of fervor. We took part in a million people march that occupied the streets leading to Central Park. Even that enormous park was not large enough to accommodate all those people. I exchanged amazed looks with Akizuki Shinichiro, a *hibakusha* and medical doctor. We had never seen such an upsurge of the anti-nuclear movement.

I had a speaking tour in some local cities with Tachibana Yuten, the director of the documentary film *"Ningen wo kaese."* We were met with warm welcomes in every city that we visited, and our audiences listened very attentively to my A-bomb experience. We also had the opportunity to lease a movie theater to show *"Ningen wo kaese."* I believe that my testimony and the visual aids helped American citizens better understand how terrible nuclear weapons are.

We must not forget an event on June 24, 1982, when

Appealing to the World to Face the Reality of the A-Bombing

hibakusha Yamaguchi Senji spoke at the UN General Assembly Special Session on Disarmament. The General Assembly Hall was open to NGOs from around the world. Holding a photo of the keloid scars that marked his body, Yamaguchi appealed, "No more wars! No more *hibakusha*!" His powerful testimony is said to have left a strong impression on government delegates and peace activists from around the world.

Although the SSD-II did not yield any of the significant results that we had expected due to strong resistance by the five nuclear powers, the one million people march as well as the *hibakushas'* vigorous activities unquestionably contributed to a shift in international opinion from "nuclear disarmament" to "the abolition of nuclear weapons."

Yamaguchi Senji addresses the UNGA SSD-II.
It was a very powerful appeal from a *hibakusha*.

Postman of Nagasaki

My frequent oversea trips led to a visit by an unexpected guest: Peter Townsend, a retired Royal Air Force Group Captain. (He died in 1995.)

Townsend, who became a writer after retirement, arranged a trip to Nagasaki in 1982 through the UN Information Centre. He told me that he wanted to write a novel about me. I had no reason to act rudely to a person who had traveled all the way to Japan. I also thought that such a novel would be of some help in making the damage and aftereffects of the atomic bombing known to the rest of the world, in particular to people in nuclear weapons possessing countries. A month-long interview began.

Townsend came to see me every day with a prefectural office employee as our interpreter. The interview would begin in the evening at my house, after I came home from the Nagasaki Telegraph Office. I had been interviewed many times since the picture of my reddened back was made public, but Townsend was the first interviewer to ask me about every detail of my life.

Townsend was a very enthusiastic interviewer. He would listen to my story for an hour and a half or two hours at a time. He occasionally had tears in his eyes. The following day he would walk around the city with a map in his hand. He walked and walked, visiting Mt. Inasa where I used to play during my childhood, the stone steps that stretch from a pier to my house, Sumiyoshi-machi where I was exposed to A-bomb radiation, and my wife's parents' home in Togitsu Town.

But working with Townsend was not without its problems. I found it difficult to make myself understood through an interpreter. After he returned home, we exchanged various stages of drafts. I found several misrepresentations, but I gave up correcting them because I was afraid I could destroy his storyline by making corrections.

I heard that the novel published in 1984 in Britain received a large public response. The book was titled "The Postman of Nagasaki" as the story was based on me, a man who was exposed to A-bomb radiation while he was delivering mail. It was soon translated into French, and its Japanese translation was published in 1985 with the title "*Nagasaki no yubinhaitatsu.*" Later, an excerpt from the novel was printed on 18 pages of a Japanese textbook published by Sanseido.

I feel grateful to Townsend for translating my thoughts into words for publication. Unfortunately, the book went out of print several years later. The Japanese edition was revived in 2005, but copies were not available in public due to copyright issues.

I have no idea how many people read my story, but I will say that I was very surprised when an American who visited me a few years ago told me that he had found a copy of the book in New Zealand.

Appearing on a French TV show

"It was right for the U.S. to drop the atomic bombs on Hiroshima and Nagasaki." "So many lives, both Japanese and American, were saved because of them." These arguments were made by American historians, scientists, and ex-servicemen in Paris in September 1985. And it left my body shaking with anger. I was with them at a discussion on a TV show. Peter Townsend, who had written the novel about me, was there too.

The French translation of "The Postman of Nagasaki" gave me the chance to appear on the French TV show. I was told that a Japanese woman living in France read the book and took it to a TV station. It then contacted me asking me to participate in an interview with Peter Townsend.

As I had just toured Europe on a Hidankyo delegation that spring, I had used up most of my paid holidays for the year. I thought I should decline the invitation, but I was compelled to change my mind in the face of the TV station's strong request. I had a tough five-day round-trip to France, accompanied by Hida Shuntaro, a medical doctor and A-bomb survivor from Hiroshima.

We arrived at the TV station to find that the program would be conducted as a debate over the question "Was the U.S. right to use the atomic bombs?" We were very surprised, since we had been led to expect the program to focus on how the book was written and published and on my reunion with Peter Townsend.

After hearing four or five American scholars make cavalier remarks, the moderator finally turned to me for comments. Stressing the fact that a single bomb killed tens of thousands of noncombatants, and that A-bomb survivors are still forced to endure such torment, I challenged them saying, "There is no justification for the use of nuclear weapons." Though I tried to be calm as I spoke about my A-bomb experience, I was boiling with anger. But I also thought it would be no use emotionally clashing with them. Without refuting what I had said, they just said that no such tragedy "must be repeated."

The moderator turned to Townsend and asked, "If you had been an American serviceman, would you have dropped an atomic bomb?" Townsend, a retired Group Captain of the RAF, said in that situation he would have done it if he had been ordered to do so. But he went on to say that it would be impossible for him to do such a terrible thing after hearing my story.

There are people who made the atomic bomb, people who ordered its production, people who ordered its use, and people who rejoiced at its use. I don't regard these people as humans. They must not be condoned, but expressions of anger cannot be the only means of making ourselves understood. I believe that only our persevering effort and appeal "We don't need to share this suffering with others," can touch the hearts of other people. That was a lesson I learned from this trip to France.

A reunion after a half century

A photograph shows painful scars on the back of my body. Part of the bone in the left arm is laid bare. The white substance that covers most of the back is zinc oxide ointment that was used to heal wounds. The medicine melted and stuck on my back due to the high fever I had. The late U.S. Marine Joe O'Donnell took this photo at a special treatment center in Shinkozen Elementary School in September 1945.

O'Donnell was 23 years old at the time. He had landed in Sasebo as a photographer for the occupation forces, and he toured Nagasaki, Hiroshima, and other places in Japan for seven months taking pictures to record the damage from the U.S. air strikes. I hear that he was deeply disturbed by the horrible scenes he witnessed in Nagasaki and Hiroshima. Soon after coming home and being discharged in the spring of 1946, he sealed off all the photo prints and negatives in a trunk.

In 1989, O'Donnell, who had been suffering from the aftereffects of his exposure to the residual radiation in Nagasaki and Hiroshima, reopened the trunk. He said he was prompted to do so after visiting a church where he saw a statue of Jesus Christ in flames making an anti-nuclear appeal. He began holding exhibitions of Hiroshima and Nagasaki A-bomb photos in various cities across the world, appealing for the elimination of nuclear weapons.

In November 1993, O'Donnell came to Nagasaki during the exhibition tour, where he visited the places that he had photographed about a half century earlier. He was surprised to learn that a boy he had photographed was alive, and he came to see me.

The photograph that O'Donnell had taken was on display in the Nagasaki International Cultural Center (now the Nagasaki Atomic Bomb Museum). I knew that the boy showing his back was me, but I did not know who had taken the picture as I was lying on my stomach. I was very surprised when he came to see me.

O'Donnell and I went to the place that had been the site of the special medical treatment center at Shinkozen Elementary School. Entering the school building, I said to O'Donnell, "This is exactly where I was taken care of." Then he said, "Yes, I took it here." He photographed my back once again and apologized, saying, "[The U.S.] did a horrible thing. I am sorry." He told me that he had deep regret and felt heartache as a man from the country that had dropped the atomic bombs.

Mr. O'Donnell passed away in 2007 at the age of 85. The pictures he left behind continue to show people how horrible nuclear weapons are.

Looking for colleagues' remains

Although I had not reached retirement age, in 1986 I quit my job after many years of service with the telegraph company. That was a year after the Nippon Telegraph and Telephone

Public Corporation was privatized to become NTT (Nippon Telegraph and Telephone Co.).

My back pain was worsening, and I was facing the limits of my physical strength. As I said earlier, I have burns from the A-bomb heat on my back, which has neither sweat glands nor sebum as it is covered with the thin skin of a scar. As the lime deposited underneath becomes bigger, it congeals in lumps and sticks out through the skin. I have had to undergo surgeries to remove the rising lumps whenever they come out.

Everyone was kind to me at the telegraph company. Whenever the office had a new director, my health conditions would be one of the items he would have to consider. No one complained about my taking leave for medical treatment, but I hated to cause trouble to my colleagues.

I decided to devote myself to the *hibakusha* movement, especially as international opinion was turning more in favor of the abolition of nuclear weapons in the aftermath of the Second Special Session of the UN General Assembly devoted to disarmament.

After retirement, I began to use my time looking for the remains of my colleagues who had died after being exposed to A-bomb radiation on that day. Many of them were irradiated near the hypocenter since the Nagasaki Motohakata Post Office, my workplace at the time, was responsible for delivering the area north of the prefectural government office. Among the 28 who were directly exposed to A-bomb radiation, I was the only survivor. Fifteen of them, whose remains were not found, were reported as missing.

One day, I learned that one of my colleagues exposed to A-bomb radiation near Ground Zero had been brought into the former Isahaya Elementary School, the same place where I was carried two days after the A-bomb attack. I went to Isahaya City to see a person who knew about those days. I was told that the colleague had died and was cremated there. I also learned that his ashes had been kept at the City Hall until they were transferred to a temple.

I went to the temple immediately but found nothing. I inquired with the temple's chief priest and benefactors about the ashes. They said, "They disappeared before we knew it." I suspected that the remains may have been transferred to Nagasaki City, since as an A-bomb victim there may have been no one to tend his grave. But I had no idea where to look. Finally, I went to the police as the last straw, but I got only a curt response. Saying, "Damn it!" to myself, I gave up on the pursuit of the colleague.

I looked for his remains for more than six months but found nothing. More than 40 years had passed since the atomic bombing. I should have begun the search sooner; I have regrets about that.

CHAPTER 9

Calling for the Expansion of Hibakusha Relief Measures

For expansion of relief measures for the hibakusha

As the movement calling for the enactment of a Hibakusha Aid Law was gaining momentum, I retired from postal work, though I had not yet reached the retirement age. In addition to the abolition of nuclear weapons, *hibakusha* have demanded passage of the Hibakusha Aid Law to provide state compensation to victims. However, to date, we have not been able to win it. In this chapter I would briefly look back on the history of our struggle calling for the expansion of official relief measures for *hibakusha*.

The *hibakusha*, who had been neglected for 12 years following the end of World War II, won the enactment of the Act for Atomic Bomb Sufferers' Medical Care (A-Bomb Medical Care Act, 1957) with our own struggle, but this law had many problems. It offered medical benefits only to those whose diseases were officially recognized as having been caused by A-bomb radiation and failed to provide any financial assistance for living expenses. So we launched a campaign to get the law revised.

ceremony hosted by Hiroshima City, then-Prime Minister Sato Eisaku said at a press conference that he had no intention to establish a comprehensive *hibakusha* aid law.

Then, Prime Minister Sato received the Nobel Peace Prize in 1974. While he did affirm the Three Non-Nuclear Principles and achieved the return of Okinawa to Japan, he was not at all a pacifist. He offered all-out support to the U.S. war in Vietnam and allowed the U.S. military to use Japan as its supply base. And since its reversion to Japan, Okinawa is still being forced to host the heavy burden of U.S. military bases.

When I went to Germany for a speaking tour, I saw a monument on which names of Nobel laureates were carved, including the name of Sato Eisaku. I asked our German friends how to write in German, and left a note there before returning to home. My note said, "This person does not deserve the prize."

Let me return to what I was saying. Nihon Hidankyo began to take actions to counter the government. In November 1973, we set up a tent in front of the Ministry of Health and Welfare and carried out a sit-in protest for five nights straight. Amid the freezing cold, we wrapped ourselves with blankets and continued the demonstration. It was our largest action, with the 3,000 people participating from all over Japan. I was engaged in logistical support, including accommodation arrangements.

Four opposition parties also made a move. They created a draft bill to provide relief to A-bomb victims and submitted it to the Upper and Lower Houses in 1974. Although the bill was scrapped, they repeatedly submitted similar bills to the Diet, and deliberations continued. As the chair of the Atomic Bomb Youth and Maidens Association of Nagasaki, I was summoned by the Diet as an unsworn witness to provide testimony. There I said to lawmakers, "These are the three points that we want the government to commit to clearly: compensation for the last 30 years of suffering that the *hibakusha* would not have had to endure without the A-bombing; protection of livelihood and health to address our anxieties; and guarantee that no more victims of nuclear weapons should be created."

Our signature campaign calling for a Hibakusha Aid Law spread nationwide. We gained momentum as many local assemblies adopted resolutions to support enactment of the law. However in 1980, the Japanese government adopted an outrageous policy: it said that the A-bomb damage must be endured.

We travelled to Tokyo many times to petition the government for the enactment of a Hibakusha Aid Law providing state compensation.

Anger over the "endurance theory"

"War damage should be equally endured by all the people of Japan." I could not believe what I was hearing from a report submitted by the Council on Basic Problems of the Atomic Bombing and Measures for the Survivors (Kihonkon). The A-bombs took the lives of tens of thousands of people and still continue to afflict so many survivors. The report told us to endure such sufferings.

Kihonkon was a private advisory body of the Health and Welfare Minister. It was established in June 1979, following the Supreme Court's decision on a lawsuit regarding the issuance of the *hibakusha* certificate to South Korean A-bomb survivors. It ruled that the A-Bomb Medical Care Act was based on an idea similar to state compensation. Thus, the government was urged to make clear whether its *hibakusha*-related measures were based on the concept of state compensation or welfare.

Seven academic expert members of the Council, including Tokyo University Professor Emeritus Kaya Seiji, worked actively and considered the opinions of Nihon Hidankyo. In April 1980, 11 *hibakusha* in Nagasaki, including myself, President Kosasa Hachiro of the Nagasaki Council of Atomic Bomb Survivors, and Watanabe Chieko, who called for peace and no nukes from her wheelchair, had the chance to present our views before the Council when it visited Nagasaki.

We were given 10 minutes each to express our feelings. I said that due to the condition of my back and scars, my life was so restricted that I could not even drown my despair in drink. I urged them not to miss this chance to enact a Hibakusha Aid Law providing state compensation. The lobby of the hotel where the meeting took place was filled with many other *hibakusha*. This showed the great expectations they had for Kihonkon.

However, the final report published by Kihonkon limited the A-bomb damage to health damage caused by radiation exposure and emphasized a balanced treatment over the A-bomb damage as opposed to general war damage. This was in line with the traditional view of the government. In our talks in Nagasaki, members of the Council seemed to have sympathy for us. It made me angry to think that they had just been pretending.

In 2010 the minutes of Kihonkon's meetings were declassified, which revealed what kind of discussion had been held. Apparently, the bureaucrats of the Health and Welfare Ministry, using financial difficulties as an excuse, tried to lead the council's discussion to adopting the "endurance theory." There was no indication in the records that other members raised any objections to them. Instead, they said that they had "wasted time" in hearing *hibakushas'* experiences and "reading long sentimental testimonies." Some criticized our call for expansion of the areas designated as affected by A-bomb radiation, saying, "It is a kind of freeloading."

The mandate of Kihonkon was to discuss the basic concept of *hibkausha*-related measures, but their deliberations were distorted by narrowing the scope of compensation for *hibkausha*. The conclusion of Kihonkon's report would be reflected on the later Hibakusha Relief Law. Kihonkon was used to endorse the government's attempt to reject national compensation and to minimize the official recognition of A-bomb damage.

Our demand for State compensation

In order to refute Kihonkon's report, Nihon Hidankyo decided to carry out a nationwide field survey on the actual situation of the *hibakusha*. We needed to reveal the truth about whether the suffering caused by the A-bombing should be regarded as damage to be endured.

The survey conducted from 1985 to 1986 covered 13,179 *hibakusha*. Our preliminary report announced at the end of 1986 showed that even 40 years later, the atomic bombs continued to torment the *hibakusha*. 30.7% of the respondents had experienced a long-term hospitalization after the A-bombing, while 51.1% had often needed outpatient treatment. As many as 42% had economic difficulty due to the atomic bombing. The survey revealed the fact that many *hibakusha* were concerned about possible death due to such radiation-related diseases as leukemia or cancers.

Hibakusha started to take action with enthusiasm. In 1987, in the "Human Chain Action with Paper Cranes," together with our supporters, we formed a human chain surrounding the Ministry of Health and Welfare building. The petition drive calling for state compensation was carried out persistently and in 1993 the number of signatures collected reached 8.14 million. Seventy-two percent of local assemblies passed resolutions in support of enactment of the Hibakusha Aid Law.

In 1993, the Liberal Democratic Party lost its majority in the General Election, and the following year a coalition government of the LDP, the Japan Socialist Party, and Sakigake (meaning forerunners in Japanese) was formed. The LDP dared to join hands with its political rival JSP just in order to stay in power. The Prime Minister of the new government was Murayama Tomiichi, the then-Chair of the JSP, who had supported a Hibakusha Aid Law to provide state compensation. This raised expectations among the *hibakusha* very high.

In 1994, the Law Concerning Atomic Bomb Survivors Relief (Hibakusha Relief Law) was enacted. This law included some positive improvements such as lifting the income limitation for receiving allowances, but as a whole it only combined the existing two laws (the Atomic Bomb Sufferers' Medical Care Law and the Special Measures Law) into one. It made no reference to state compensation, and all in all it was a product of compromise.

Although the Prime Minister was from the Socialist Party, the government remained essentially led by the LDP. Once they joined the ruling coalition, the JSP reversed every policy it had held and rapidly lost the support of the people. Mr. Murayama resigned only a year and a half later. I still want to ask him, "What on earth did you want to do in the government?"

There were some *hibakusha* who left the movement after the Hibakusha Relief Law was established. No doubt, thanks to our persistent efforts, we have achieved great improvement in *hibakusha* measures, such as removing the burden of our medical fees. However, our fundamental demand for state compensation is yet to be achieved.

You may wonder why we are so adamant. We believe that the only way to prevent atomic bombings or wars in the future is by making the government acknowledge its responsibility for the war and compensate for war damage. We also believe it is our duty to achieve this task.

Lawsuits for official recognition on A-bomb diseases

Matsuya Hideko stood surrounded by the media and ringing applause, all smiles in front of the TV camera at the Nagasaki District Court in May 1993. She had filed a lawsuit in which she appealed for the reversal of the government's decision to deny her application for the official recognition of her medical condition as A-bomb-induced disease. The Nagasaki District Court upheld her claim and acknowledged her disorders as the result of radiation from the atomic bombing.

The government has always tried to underestimate the damage from the A-bombing, and the official recognition system of A-bomb diseases was typical of the state's approach. The government recognized A-bomb diseases only when *hibakusha* had "injury or illness caused by radiation" or "difficulty recovering from injury or illness due to the effects of radiation," and systematically dismissed the claims of the *hibakusha* who were exposed to the atomic bombing outside the 2km radius of the blast center as "not having been affected by radiation."

Ms. Matsuya was one such *hibakusha*. At age 3, she was exposed to the A-bombing at home, located 2.45 km from ground zero. A roof tile blown by the blast hit her hard on her head, which paralyzed the right side of her body. The injury did not heal easily and took two and a half years to close. Severe headaches continued and often made her "feel like just throwing away [her] head." She applied for A-bomb disease recognition twice but was turned down both times. In 1988, she decided to file a lawsuit against the government.

This was a time when we felt strong public backing toward the enactment of the Hibakusha Aid Law, and as many as 9,000 people across the country supported the lawsuit. Yamaguchi Senji, the then-President of Nagasaki Hisaikyo, represented the "Association to Support the Matsuya Lawsuit". I was the Vice President of Hisaikyo at the time, and of course I was one of the members of the Support Association.

With the government's appeal, the next stage was set at the

Fukuoka High Court. Every time a court hearing took place we hired a bus and left Nagasaki early in the morning with Ms. Matsuya and her supporters on board. I often loaded banners and other materials in my car and followed the bus. Standing beside a rally where Mr. Yamaguchi and others spoke through the loudspeaker, I called on the people passing by to support the lawsuit.

At the High Court, our lawyers knocked down every argument the government raised and won a victorious ruling. The government appealed the case to the Supreme Court, and finally in July 2000, the victory of Matsuya's case was confirmed at the highest level. Attorney Nakamura Naosato, who was in charge of the Matsuya case said, "The government has systematically turned down *hibakushas'* applications, using a formula which estimates the exposed dose according to the distance from ground zero as the only yardstick. But the court declared a clear 'No' to this practice and urged the government to make decisions based on the particular circumstances of the individual *hibakusha*."

We expected that based on the ruling the government would amend the faulty administration of the A-bomb disease recognition system. Yet, to our amazement the government made even stricter criteria for the *hibakusha* screening. This triggered the start of the *hibakushas'* collective lawsuits to correct the government policy.

Achievement of the collective lawsuits

Hibakusha won victory after victory in the collective lawsuits seeking official recognition of their A-bomb-induced medical conditions. Since their first filing against the government in 2003 in response to the call made by the lawyers' group, *hibakusha* have marked 19 victorious court rulings in succession.

For a long time, the government had dismissed the claims of the *hibakusha* based on the DS 86 (Dosimetry System 86) formula which estimated the exposed dose of each *hibakusha*'s radiation according to the distance from ground zero. As of 2003, the number of *hibakusha* who had been recognized as A-bomb disease patients was only 2,200, accounting for less than 1% of the then 270,000 *hibakusha*.

It generally took a long time after filing an application to receive the government's eligibility decision. If a *hibakusha* filed a petition of objection, it would take several more years before a final decision was made. Even if a *hibakusha* brought a case to court and won, the government would appeal it to a higher court. We often thought that the government was just waiting for the time when all the *hibakusha* would die off.

Nationwide, a total of 306 *hibakusha* joined the collective lawsuits as plaintiffs. While the abolition of nuclear weapons was not achieved, nor was a Hibakusha Aid Law to provide state compensation, at the very least the *hibakusha* seemed to have a common desire to fight back against the government. Nihon Hidankyo and Nagasaki Hisaikyo offered their full support to these lawsuits.

It was around the time these lawsuits began that Yamaguchi Senji withdrew from the frontline of the Hibakusha movement. His health had declined and he had to move from Nagasaki City to a nursing home in Unzen City. This increased the opportunities for me to take his place speaking at rallies and in meetings.

Suffering from consecutive legal defeats, the government loosened the criteria for granting the A-bomb disease recognition in 2008 and 2009. It announced that those who were exposed to the A-bombs within a 3.5km radius and suffered from any one of seven diseases, including cancer, should be positively recognized. And in August 2009, then-Prime Minister Aso Taro made a political decision to withdraw the government's appeals to higher courts, to certify those victorious plaintiffs in the lower courts as having A-bomb induced diseases, and also to make a one-time payment to the plaintiffs who lost in the lower courts. Thus, we achieved a victory against the government.

In December 2010, based on the agreement signed between the government and Nihon Hidankyo, the Ministry of Health and Labour set up a working group to review the A-bomb disease recognition system. Among the members were two Nihon Hidankyo representatives, in addition to academics and lawyers. The group met regularly, but was not able to come up with any positive results due to the government's resistance.

Since then, many *hibakushas'* applications for A-bomb disease recognition have been rejected, even under the new screening criteria. Even when a *hibakusha* suffers from an illnesses listed among those for positive recognition, the government has continued to turn down the application, saying, "The causality from the bomb radiation cannot be recognized." The fundamental stance of the government to underestimate the damage from the atomic bombing remains unchanged. My earnest desire is to achieve, as soon as possible, a system through which all the *hibakusha* can benefit from the relief measures.

Note: Around the end of 2013, the Japanese government introduced a new criteria for A-bomb disease recognition. Regarding the three non-cancer illnesses (cardiac infarction, hypothyroidism, and chronic hepatitis/cirrhosis), it removed the condition of "radiation causality," which had been the major cause for dismissed applications as a consequence of hibakushas' difficulty in providing proof. At the same time, the government narrowed the scope of coverage for positive recognition by changing the distance from ground zero of directly exposed hibakusha from a 3.5km radius to 2.0km. In a new lawsuit filed by the hibakusha whose applications were denied under the new criteria, in 2014, the Kumamoto District Court ruled in favor of the hibakusha. As this shows, the gap between the government administration and judiciary has not been bridged. Hibakusha continue to claim that fundamental revision of the A-bomb recognition system is necessary.

Feeling frustrated by the working group's review, which took so long to reach any conclusion, in spring 2013, Nihon Hidankyo conducted a national action to lobby the parliamentarians.

CHAPTER 10:

Road to the Abolition of Nuclear Weapons

Logic of the massive nuclear country: U.S.A.

I have spoken about my A-bomb experience 23 times outside Japan. The country I have visited most frequently is the United States, where I have traveled nine times. It is the only country that has ever used atomic bombs, and it is also the key country for achieving the elimination of nuclear weapons. However, it is so difficult to appeal for the abolition of nuclear weapons in the U.S. I would now like to touch on the situation regarding nuclear weapons in U.S. and globally after the Cold War.

"I basically think that President Truman made the right decision when he used the Bomb on Hiroshima." Former U.S. Secretary of Defense Dick Cheney made this astonishing remark in 1991, when public opinion calling for nuclear disarmament was growing with the end of the Cold War. The statement came shortly after the U.S.-led Coalition Forces launched massive air strikes against Iraq in the Gulf War triggered by the Iraqi invasion of Kuwait. It was understood that with this comment he implied that the use of nuclear weapons was an option at that time.

Then-President George H. W. Bush did not correct the Defense Secretary's comment. Instead he also defended the decision to drop the atomic bombs, stating, "No apology is required." The scar on my back ached and my mind went blank with anger. After 45 years, they still support matter-of-factly the use of the weapon that massacred innocent citizens. Needless to say, the *hibakusha* stood up in protest all across the country.

In an effort to appeal to the *hibakusha* living in the U.S. to raise their voices in solidarity with us, Nihon Hidankyo sent me to St. George, Utah in 1993. Located about 200 km (124 miles) from the Nevada Test Site, the city was blanketed with a massive amount of radioactive fallout.

A radiation monitor was installed, which is unusual for a small city like St. George to have. I heard that the actor John Wayne died of cancer due to his exposure to radiation while shooting a Western film nearby. Many citizens had cancers or leukemia, and one man that I met had to sell his house to pay the fees for his child's medical treatment. I asked the residents if they ever thought of demanding compensation from the government, but I could see the resigned look on their faces. We all shared the aspiration that no one else should suffer the damage caused by nuclear weapons, but I could tell how difficult it was for those in the U.S. to raise their voices.

I faced the same sort of problem again in 1995. The Smithsonian National Air and Space Museum in Washington, D.C. planned to hold an atomic bomb exhibition, but strong protests came from U.S. veterans and conservative legislators, and the museum scaled back the original plan and changed it to an "Enola Gay Exhibition," using the name of the B-29 bomber that dropped the atomic bomb on Hiroshima. Nagasaki City was going to lend A-bomb photos and materials, including the picture of my wounded back, but this was also cancelled. Later, I learned that there was no exhibition of items depicting the damage caused by the atomic bombs, and that the whole message of the display was that the "atomic bombing hastened the end of the war."

The A-bomb exhibit planned by the Smithsonian National Air and Space Museum was changed to an exhibition on Enola Gay, the B-29 bomber that dropped the A-bomb.

Disseminating the facts through civilian exchanges

The Smithsonian Institution's "Atomic bomb exhibition" was cancelled because of the pressures from veterans and Congress members. However, another "A-bomb exhibition" was proposed to be held at American University, also in Washington D.C.

The purpose of the exhibition was to examine the historic

significance of the atomic bombing through A-bomb materials of Hiroshima and Nagasaki. The university's plan contrasted sharply with the Smithsonian's. The exhibit was held as part of the university's summer session, and the items displayed included a charred lunch box, a melted rosary, and photos taken immediately after the bombing.

I learned that Ms. Naono Akiko, a second generation *hibakusha* who was a staff member at American University at the time (currently associate professor at Kyushu University), worked very hard to make the exhibit possible. This A-bomb exhibit, which was realized by the effort of citizens, motivated others to hold exhibitions in other countries as well.

In an effort to make the facts of the atomic bombing widely known, I engaged in civilian exchanges from the mid- to late-1980s at my home. I hosted several reporters from the U.S. who were invited by the Hiroshima International Cultural Foundation to report in the U.S. on the A-bomb damage suffered by the *hibakusha* and on their earnest wish for the elimination of nuclear weapons. This project was named the "Akiba Project," as it was initiated by Mr. Akiba Tadatoshi. At the time, Mr. Akiba was an associate professor at Tufts University in the U.S. He later served as Mayor of Hiroshima.

During their stay in Nagasaki, the reporters heard my story and visited the Nagasaki Atomic Bomb Museum. They all were astonished by the magnitude of the damage caused by the A-bomb. They said that in the U.S. many people supported the A-bombing, but the public knew little about the reality of the damage the bomb had caused. As they took pictures of my back, I was glad to hear those reporters say enthusiastically that they wanted to disseminate the truth in their country.

During the project period from 1979 to 1988, a total of 34

reporters came to Nagasaki, and I hear that some of them have continued to report on the nuclear damage. Now that it is difficult for the aging *hibakusha* to go abroad for speaking tours, nothing is more encouraging than to see U.S. citizens calling for the abolition of nuclear weapons.

One thing does worry me; it is about a reporter who stayed in my home. After going back to the U.S., he sent me a letter saying that he had lost his job. He wrote that when he reported the facts of the A-bomb damage, his boss yelled at him, "Are you really American?" and the boss fired him. He did nothing wrong. I feel very sorry for him. I wonder what he is up to now.

Stomped wreath

Apart from the statement by the U.S. president justifying the A-bombing, there was another occasion during which the country trampled over the *hibakushas'* feelings. In September 1989, the *USS Rodney M. Davis*, suspected of carrying nuclear weapons, called at Nagasaki port.

We were filled with rage. For the *hibakusha*, who lost their family members to the A-bomb and endured great suffering from the aftereffects of exposure to radiation, the port call of a U.S. warship, possibly loaded with nuclear weapons, was just unacceptable. We immediately urged the prefectural authorities in charge of the Nagasaki port to refuse the port call, and we also requested the U.S. Consulate in Fukuoka to cancel it. Yet the *USS Davis* came into the port as if it was its own, while some 400 people, including *hibakusha*, packed the Matsugae Pier shouting, "Get out!" in protest.

The following day the captain and other crewmembers of the *Davis* were supposed to visit the Peace Park to offer flowers.

Without apologizing for dropping the atomic bomb and after coming into the city in a warship suspected of carrying nuclear weapons, they claimed that they were coming to "pay tribute to the victims." They actually dishonored the victims. With Mr. Yamaguchi Senji, the then-President of the Nagasaki Atomic Bomb Survivors Council taking the lead, we staged a sit-in in front of the Peace Statute. The uniformed captain came toward us intimidatingly. Not allowing myself to be provoked, I held my body trembled with anger.

The captain laid a wreath before the statute and walked away. The foot of a photographer who went after him hit the wreath and it fell off. That moment, Senji shouted, "This cannot be a tribute!" He then trampled the wreath. Two *hibakusha* who had lost their family members to the Bomb followed him, stomping on the wreath over and over.

They faced strong criticism from Nagasaki citizens for what they did. But all the *hibakusha* who were there shared the same feeling. I regret that I did not join Senji and the other two; if all of us had trampled on the wreath they would not have had to bear the brunt of blame.

We learned that the purpose of *Davis'* port call was resupply and rest. Why did they choose Nagasaki instead of Sasebo, where the U.S. military base was located? To me, it did not make any sense. If they had in fact wanted to offer flowers to console the souls of the victims, they should have instead attended the Peace Memorial Ceremony that's held every summer. It was not until 2011, more than 65 years after the end of the war, that the U.S. government sent a representative to the memorial ceremony for the first time.

We do not hate the U.S. We hate nuclear weapons. We did resent the U.S. before, but we have overcome resentment and bitterness, and we are working so that there will never be another *hibakusha*. I wonder why it's so difficult for them to understand how we feel.

Advisory opinion of the International Court of Justice

Showing the photo panel of a charred boy at the International Court of Justice (ICJ) in The Hague, Netherlands in November 1995, the late Ito Iccho, Mayor of Nagasaki at that time, asked "What crime did these children commit?" Iccho gave an oral statement as the witness for the Japanese government at the ICJ, which was examining whether the use of nuclear weapons violates international law.

The ICJ heard the case following requests by the World Health Organization (WHO) and U.N. General Assembly for an advisory opinion on the question of whether the use of nuclear weapons would be a breach of obligations under international law. This occurred on the eve of the 50th anniversary of the atomic bombing, as NGOs were strengthening the call for the abolition of nuclear weapons.

In 1996, the ICJ handed down a landmark advisory opinion, stating that, "the threat and use of nuclear weapons would generally be contrary to the rules of international law." For the *hibakusha* this was a matter of course, but this was the first time that these inhumane weapons were judged in the light of international law. However, the ICJ avoided deciding on the legality of the use of nuclear weapons in an extreme circumstance of self-defense, in which the very survival of a State would be at stake. Seven of the 14 judges were said to have avoided making a judgement on this question, but one judge maintained that the use or threat of use of nuclear weapons is "illegal in any circumstances whatsoever."

The judge was Christopher Weeramantry from Sri Lanka. He came to Nagasaki after he retired from office, and I guided him around the city with Yamaguchi Senji. After visiting the Nagasaki Atomic Bomb Museum, he encouraged us saying, "Coming to this museum, anyone can understand the horror of nuclear weapons. Please continue to send out messages from Nagasaki." The ICJ advisory opinion issued by the judges, including Mr. Weeramantry, gave the *hibakusha*, NGOs, and the countries advocating anti-nuclear policies encouragement to put even more pressure on the nuclear weapon states.

The 2000 NPT Review Conference took place amidst this favorable development. Despite the fact that India and Pakistan, the two countries that had by this point embarked on nuclear weapons programs, remained outside the treaty, the NPT is the only binding commitment in a multilateral treaty to the goal of disarmament by the five nuclear-weapons States and to prohibit the rest of the states from possessing nuclear weapons. The state parties meet every five years at a Review Conference to assess the implementation of the treaty. In 2000, the Review Conference for the first time referred to the elimination of nuclear weapons.

The final document adopted by consensus included a call for an "unequivocal undertaking by the nuclear-weapon States to accomplish the total elimination of their nuclear arsenals." Fifty-five years after the A-bombing, we thought we finally caught a glimpse of a path toward the abolition of nuclear weapons. But we were soon disillusioned.

Still a long way to go toward eliminating nuclear weapons

After the successful 2000 NPT Review Conference and other positive developments, it seemed that the world was undoubtedly on the path towards abolishing nuclear weapons. However, the situation completely turned around the following year.

On September 11, 2001, a dreadful incident shook the world. Two airplanes crashed into the Twin Towers of the World Trade Center in New York City in simultaneous terrorist attacks that took the lives of many innocent people. Terrorism must not be condoned for any reason whatsoever. But the way the U.S. responded to the attacks seemed extreme. President George W. Bush instantly declared "retaliation", and the following month launched an invasion into Afghanistan in an effort to chase down of the terrorists responsible for the 9-11 attacks. With its overwhelming military power, the U.S. forces ousted the Taliban regime and remained in the country. The Bush administration went on to denounce Iran, Iraq, and the Democratic People's Republic of Korea (DPRK), labeling them the "Axis of Evil" and "terrorist states possessing weapons of mass destruction." In 2003, the U.S. went to war in Iraq in complete disregard of international opinion.

The Bush administration also unilaterally withdrew from the Anti-Ballistic Missile Treaty with Russia, refused to ratify the Comprehensive Test Ban Treaty (CTBT), and spoke of developing mini-nukes.

Alarmed by these moves, we *hibakusha*, old as we were, devoted ourselves to the movement. In the run-up to the 2005 NPT Review Conference, I attended the NPT Preparatory Committee held at the UN Headquarters in New York in 2004. There I spoke before ambassadors from different countries on behalf of the Nagasaki Atomic Bomb Survivors Council to call for the elimination of nuclear weapons.

At the meeting, I saw the confrontation between the nuclear weapons haves and have-nots. The U.S. was exposed to severe criticism for its attempt to limit the peaceful activities of nuclear energy by non-nuclear weapon states while neglecting its nuclear disarmament responsibilities. I was astonished when the Japanese ambassador to the UN told me that it was thanks to the U.S. nuclear umbrella that Japan had not been attacked by North Korea. I understood that the DPRK was carrying forward on its nuclear program, but with his remarks the ambassador sounded like he was just a mouthpiece for the U.S. rather than the representative of the A-bombed country.

Meanwhile the 2005 NPT Review Conference started. *Hibakusha* from Nagasaki, including myself and Ms. Shimohira Sakue, who was an eloquent storyteller about her A-bomb experience, participated in a series of events. We carried a banner as we marched from the vicinity of the UN Headquarters to Central Park. As we walked, I distributed my name cards with the photo of my scarred red back printed on them to people on the street, and I spoke about the absurdity of the use or threat of nuclear weapons.

As we feared, the Review Conference mostly spun its wheels, getting nowhere due to the confrontation between the nuclear weapon states and non-nuclear weapon states. It failed to produce any outcome and turned out to be a big setback from the previous 2000 Review Conference and its successful adoption of a final document.

Marching with Shimohira Sakue on the streets of New York City, carrying the banner: "Abolish All Nuclear Weapons"

Nominated for the Nobel Peace Prize

The NPT Review Conference in May 2005 betrayed the expectations of the *hibakusha* and everyone who hopes for a world without nuclear weapons. But we took this opportunity to talk with a wide range of U.S. citizens and various government representatives about the consequences that the use of nuclear weapons would cause. Particularly significant, we were able to give an A-bomb exhibition for the first time inside the UN headquarters building in New York.

Nihon Hidankyo hosted the exhibition, which was on display for about three weeks during the conference. Mounted in the lobby and underground passageway at the UN building, 30 photo panels depicted Hiroshima and Nagasaki just after the A-bombings, including a photograph of myself with the back burnt red, a photo that has become well-known all over the world since it was carried in a newspaper in 1970.

Nihon Hidankyo had tried for several years to hold such an exhibition, including my picture, during UN meetings. But UN staff had denied the request saying that the images "are too cruel for display." We argued back that we shouldn't close our eyes to what actually had happened in Nagasaki and Hiroshima. After arduous negotiations, the exhibition was finally organized in 2005. Alongside the exhibition was a space for the *hibakusha* to give testimonies about their experiences, through which many visitors came to better understand what the A-bomb survivors had suffered.

We met and talked, not only with government representatives attending the conference at the UN, but with U.S. citizens across the country as well. At the time, the Iraq War plodded along after it was started against international public opinion. This may be one of the reasons people listened to us with such earnestness.

Good news arrived suddenly in late 2005, seven months after we had returned home. At the award ceremony of the Nobel Peace Prize, Nihon Hidankyo was praised by name. Nobel Prize Committee Chair Ole Danbolt Mjøs said, "The atom bombs fell on Hiroshima and Nagasaki 60 years ago. Since then, the world has been united in the wish that nothing like that must ever happen again."

Until then, Nihon Hidankyo had been nominated for the prize at least five times. Although we missed out on the award once again, at this moment our activities were finally recognized by the world. We heard that the committee valued the *hibakusha* for our persistent calls for the abolition of nuclear weapons despite our untold suffering from the aftereffects of the A-bombings, as well as for our vigorous efforts after September 11, 2001.

Since then, Nihon Hidankyo has been nominated for the prize several more times, but it has yet to be awarded the prize. Needless to say, our campaign is not for the prize, but I am sure that a Nobel Peace Prize for Nihon Hidankyo would encourage the anti-nuclear weapons movement around the world.

Arrival of President Obama

In April 2009, I was unable to take my eyes off the TV program broadcasting a speech by President Barack Obama, the first African-American president in U.S. history. He said in Prague, "the United States will take concrete steps toward a world without nuclear weapons."

After the September 11, 2001 attacks, the United States went against the global currents toward nuclear disarmament. Amid growing concern over nuclear proliferation, North Korea finally succeeded in conducting a nuclear weapon test in 2006. We felt increasingly powerless as we campaigned to "make Nagasaki the last A-bombed city."

Then, President Obama arrived. In the past, some U.S. presidents had publicly justified the atomic bombings, but he was different. He showed his determination to achieve a world without nuclear weapons, saying, "As the only nuclear power to have used a nuclear weapon, the United States has a moral responsibility to act." I felt as if our sense of despair over the past several years disappeared. But our joy was not without reservation, as our expectations had been betrayed so many times before. Therefore, we remained worried that he might compromise his position.

One month after Obama's speech in Prague, 17 Nobel Peace Prize laureates issued the "Hiroshima-Nagasaki Declaration" to appeal to governments and citizens across the world to take action for the elimination of nuclear weapons. We heard that the declaration was intended to keep up the momentum President Obama created through his Prague speech, building toward the NPT Review Conference the following year. This encouraged us because the declaration praised the *hibakusha* for our role in helping to prevent the use of nuclear weapons after World War II.

If nobody had survived the A-bombings of Hiroshima and Nagasaki, by now there would be many countries in the world with their names on the map, but without any people. Nuclear weapons have been produced for actual use, but have never been used since 1945 because A-bomb survivors, through their painstaking struggle have appealed to the world that nuclear weapons should never be used again.

In December 2009, President Obama was awarded the Nobel Peace Prize, although he had made no concrete achievements regarding peace. A-bomb survivors who have been working hard for more than half a century had mixed feelings, but we considered this as an expression of high expectations by the world's people for a nuclear-weapon-free world.

As the 2010 NPT Review Conference approached, I became increasingly determined to go to the United States by any means possible. I was 80 years old, and I thought this might be my last visit to the United States. The world was changing with the advent of President Obama. As a man whose life was ruined by the A-bombing, I wanted to see with my own eyes the moment that the course would be set toward the abolition of nuclear weapons.

Appeal at the NPT Review Conference

In April 2010, one month before the NPT Review Conference, it was decided that I, representing Nihon Hidankyo, would make a speech at the conference to be held at the U.N. in New York. It was an important opportunity for an NGO representative to make a direct appeal to governments around the world. I was very nervous, but I was determined to take on the mission, thinking that taking this stage would probably be the grand finale for my life.

I drafted the speech, making some modifications on what I usually would tell the school trip students: That I was blown away by the blast while I was delivering postal mail, and that my entire back was terribly burned by the heat lays and radiation; that I stayed in bed for one year and 9 months, lying face down and crying, "Kill me!" out of agony; and that even to this day, I suffer from lingering pains in my back that hamper me from sleeping soundly. I had only one thought in my mind: I must make every possible effort to appeal to the nuclear weapon states about all the truths of the suffering caused by nuclear weapons that can never be healed by such words as "It must have been tough on you."

The trip would take about half a day from Narita (Tokyo International Airport) to New York City. Due to the pain in my back, I would not be able to lean on the backrest of the aircraft seat. It was a routine condition for me in every trip overseas. But still, I was old and it was very difficult, just as I had expected. But my mind was set on delivering the speech.

Finally, May 7 arrived. The conference hall of the United Nations has 400 seats, and most of them were filled by official government delegates or NGO representatives. I recognized the government officers of nuclear powers such as the United

States, Russia, and France were also present. As my turn approached, I could not keep my anger from growing inside me. Even 65 years after the atomic bombings, there are still people clinging onto nuclear weapons.

In my hand, I held up the photo of me with my burned red back taken in January 1946. I told my story of experiencing the A-bombing, and concluded with the deepest conviction of my heart: "Nuclear weapons are weapons of annihilation. They can never coexist with human beings." With President Obama entering presidential office, the U.S. and Russia agreed on a new Strategic Arms Reduction Treaty to reduce their strategic nuclear warheads to the lowest level in history, but it was far from achieving the abolition of nuclear weapons. If a single weapon is left, there remains a possibility that somebody may experience what I've gone through. I wanted to make sure that they understood that.

When I finished the 12-minute speech, the floor was filled with applause until I walked back to my seat. Later I learned that officials from Russia said that my speech had reminded them of the nuclear threat once again, and that Russia must work towards drastic nuclear disarmament with the U.S. and other nuclear weapon states. I felt I did everything I could. With this sentiment, I decided to wait and observe the discussion in the NPT Review Conference.

Has the world changed yet?

The NPT Review Conference was held in May 2010. We returned to Japan several days after I made the speech in front of the government representatives from around the world. The week of activities in the U.S. was over, and now we would observe the progress of the conference from Nagasaki.

The focus was around whether the concrete timetable towards the abolition of nuclear weapons which was included in the first draft would be included in the final document. Ultimately, the timetable was not included. I think there was a bit of progress, as the agreed final document reaffirmed the "unequivocal undertaking for the abolition of nuclear weapons" which was established in 2000, and it said that the efforts toward the abolition of nuclear weapons "will be reported in 2014". But honestly, I must admit that I was expecting more than that.

That summer, the A-bombed cities suddenly became centers of attention when Mr. Ban Ki-moon, the Secretary-General of the United Nations, made his first visit to Nagasaki on August 5. Mr. Ban was advocating for a nuclear weapons convention to place a total ban on the possession and development of such weapons by any state. I guided him through the Nagasaki Atomic Bomb Museum and gave a brief explanation of what the atomic bombing did to me in front of my red back photo.

Mr. Ban listened intently and took notes. I think he thought that he could strengthen and maintain his conviction by visiting the A-bombed cities. You see, we never had a Secretary-General of the United Nations who advocated and took action for the abolition of nuclear weapons before him. "I wish you all the best in your work" I said, and we shock hands. Later, Mr. Ban dedicated a wreath at the memorial of the atomic explosion's epicenter, and declared before the souls of the victims, "The only way to ensure that such weapons will never again be used is to eliminate them all."

The next day, on August 6, Mr. Ban attended the Hiroshima Peace Memorial Ceremony together with the U.S. Ambassador to Japan John Roos. It was the first time that the Ambassador of the United States, the country that dropped the A-bombs, attended the ceremony. Representatives of Great Britain and France were also present for the first time. The media described this as a sign of growing momentum for nuclear abolition, and wrote "the world may be seeing a change."

Three years have passed since then. There are some talks between the United States and Russia for further nuclear disarmament, but no movement towards abolition can be seen. Even under the Obama administration, which called for "the peace and security of a world without nuclear weapons," sub-critical nuclear testing is still taking place to keep nuclear weapons ready to be used at any time.

There are nations who cling onto nuclear weapons. There are nations who want to possess nuclear weapons to achieve diplomatic superiority. This framework has not yet changed. This is so frustrating. I already lost many of my fellow *hibakusha* who kept on saying, "I cannot die until I see all nuclear weapons abolished." I wonder when the day will come when the *hibakusha* can die peacefully with the assurance that "the world has finally changed."

"I wish you all the best in your work towards the abolition of nuclear weapons," I told Mr. Ban Ki-moon, the Secretary-General of the United Nations, as we shook hands.

CHAPTER 11

Before We Hand over Our Work to Descendants

Death of Sen-chan

"Just one last time, I wanted to spend some time to talk with you." I offered an incense stick and talked to him in the photograph. Yamaguchi Senji, who had led the *hibakusha* movement for a long time, passed away in July 2013 at the age of 82. As I looked at the photos from his youth, with a nostalgic feeling and the unbearable sentiment of losing a precious friend, my eyes welled up with tears.

I met Senji-san at the former Omura Naval Hospital where both of us were hospitalized right after the bombing. Later, we met again in Nagasaki City, and he invited me to join the anti-nuclear movement. We had worked together ever since the establishment of the Nagasaki A-Bomb Youth Association in 1955. Senji-san, who had been burned badly on upper half of his front body, and I, who had been burned on the back, had a strong sense of comradeship, as both of us survived the direct bombing.

Senji-san was honest with his feelings and a man of action. In

1954, when he had found that *hibakushas'* medical costs were not covered by the government but by donation, he became angry and traveled from Nagasaki to Tokyo by train without paying to petition at the National Diet Building. However, he went to Tokyo without having done any research only to find that the Diet was in recess. I heard that story later and we laughed at his recklessness.

Since he often took actions on a sudden impulse, we had conflicts a number of times. But the next day, he would seem as if nothing had happened. This frustrated me, as I would think, "How can he forget what he has said?" But that was also one of his charms. Everybody called him "Sen-chan," and liked him.

I came onto the stage of the anti-nuclear movement only after 1970, when the photograph of my red back appeared in public. But Senji-san led the movement over time. His anger toward the A-bomb supported and motivated him. In 1982, he was the first *hibakusha* to make a speech for the abolition of nuclear weapons at the United Nations. He looked so amazingly powerful.

Ten years ago, Senji-san's health deteriorated, and he moved to a nursing home for the elderly in Unzen City. Since then, people have asked me to speak in his place more frequently than before. I became the President of Nagasaki Council of A-Bomb Survivors (Nagasaki Hisaikyo) in 2006, and I took over the position as one of the co-chairpersons of the Japan Confederation of A-and H-Bomb Sufferers Organizations (Nihon Hidankyo) from him in 2010. I don't think I'm the right person to take such leadership, but the situation made me do so.

When I heard the news of his death, I felt discouraged and feared that I might be next. However, I made a promise to his wife, "I will do my best as long as I can move." I don't think I can work like Senji-san, but given that the photo of my red back is well known to the world, I must play the role as a representative figure of the *hibakusha*.

I want to say to Sen-chan in heaven, "You did a great job. Now, have a good rest."

Failure in health, anxiety, and my last word

I used to tell my story to students on school trips more than 300 times a year, but the number of my lectures has decreased noticeably. I fell sick in the beginning of 2012 and was hospitalized for three months with acute pneumonia. I used to weigh 47 kg, but now my weight has fallen to 44 kg. I can't regain my strength.

In May 2012, shortly after I was discharged from the hospital, I went through surgery to remove a hard lump on my back. It had to be removed by gouging a scalpel into flesh. Every time I have a surgery, the open wound has to be covered by a piece of skin taken from my leg or buttocks because the cicatrix covering my back would tear if pulled together. Up to now I have had 24 such operations, and my back has become like a patchwork quilt.

Even in such a health condition, people ask me to give lectures. I would like to do this as long as I am able to, but now my voice fails me. I have never been able to speak in a loud voice, but after the pneumonia, deep breathing is difficult and makes me cough. So I now limit the number of lectures that I give to 20 to 30 a year.

I show photos of my red back and other images while I'm talking, and I keep standing when I deliver talks so the children sitting in the rear can also see them. Recently, I often tell the students, "Please listen to my story as my last word, and remember it deep in your heart." And I add, "Please pass this story on to other people on my behalf."

Sixty-eight years have passed since that day. Children of today have a totally different history, background, and lifestyle. I sometimes wonder how much they understand my story. But we are all humans, so I'm sure they have the compassion to understand other people's pain. I believe that and continue the lectures because I don't know how many more years I can live. I want to reach as many people as I can to convey the aspirations of the *hibakusha*, so that no more people should suffer like us.

When I finish a lecture, I sit in the back room of Nagasaki Hisaikyo where I serve as president and have a smoke. My family gets angry, saying, "You will get pneumonia again!" but I cannot quit smoking.

About 65 years ago, when I was hospitalized in the former Omura Naval Hospital, I had a fever of 42 degrees Celsius (107 degrees Fahrenheit) for three days. Nothing worked, and even the doctors gave up. However, when I smoked a cigarette that a man who was staying in the same room gave me, the fever abated. Everyone was surprised. Since then I've been smoking for good luck. It soothes my lungs and makes me feel better.

Accident at Fukushima Daiichi Nuclear Power Plant

On March 11, 2011, a huge earthquake struck Eastern Japan. The tsunami caused by the earthquake swallowed many towns and roads, and the number of dead or missing was nearly 20,000. The wreckage in the areas struck by the disaster reminded me of the ruins after the bombing in Nagasaki.

The accident at Fukushima Daiichi Nuclear Power Station subsequently occurred. The reactor building exploded, and a massive amount of radioactive substance was discharged in the air. "My worst fear has turned into reality," I thought.

Why does Japan, the country that experienced the atomic bombing, depend on nuclear power generation? This has been my question for a long time. I knew from my experience that nuclear energy or weapons cannot coexist with humans. However, *hibakusha* did not raise opposition when construction plans for nuclear power plants began in the mid-1950s.

I think everyone was deceived by the words, "peaceful use of nuclear energy." In the founding proclamation of Nihon Hidankyo, which was established in 1956, you can find a phrase as follows: "Atomic power, which has a tendency to follow the road to destruction and extermination, must absolutely [be] converted to a servant for the happiness and prosperity of humankind. This is the only desire we hold as long as we live."

Five months after the Fukushima nuclear power plant accident, Nihon Hidankyo changed its position and now advocates the abandonment of nuclear power generation. I think *hibakusha* had not opposed nuclear power generation because they wanted to concentrate on realizing the total abolition of nuclear weapons and winning the Hibakusha Aid Law providing for state compensation. Of course there were some *hibakusha* who were working in nuclear power industry, so if we had touched upon the nuclear power generation issue, our movement might have been split.

As for myself, I have never thought that peaceful use of nuclear power would be possible. I was a vocal opponent for a while, but gradually quieted down about this issue. As the nuclear power plants were constructed one by one, scholars and the press increasingly stopped opposing to them. I heard that the government scattered money to prefectures and municipalities where nuclear power plants were located so that local residents would hold their tongues. In time, I gave up, thinking that my action alone would not change anything.

We now know that the government will underestimate the effects of the Fukushima accident just as it downplayed the radiation damage of the atomic bomb. Nothing will be done if we are silent; again people must cry out for help and relief from the government.

We suffer from the atomic bombs that were used in the war Japan started, and the people in Fukushima suffer from the nuclear power plant accident that was caused by policies promoted by the government. We share the same root cause of our afflictions. I hope we can take actions hand in hand.

Meeting with Truman's grandson

In the summer of 2012, Clifton Truman Daniel, 56, visited the two atom-bombed cities. His grandfather was former U.S. President Truman, who gave the order to drop the atomic bombs on Hiroshima and Nagasaki. When I first heard about his visit, I felt a sense of caution.

He was invited by Mr. Sasaki Masahiro, whose sister Sasaki Sadako is represented in the form of a sculpture at the Children's Peace Monument in the Hiroshima Peace Park. I heard that Masahiro came across Daniel in 2010 when he visited the site of the World Trade Center Building in New York City which had been attacked on September 11, 2001.

Daniel visited Nagasaki City after Hiroshima City in August 2012. He was accompanied by the man whose grandfather was a radar operator on board the B-29 that dropped the A-bomb. I was supposed to tell them about my A-bomb experience.

I met them in the Nagasaki National Peace Memorial Hall for the Atomic Bomb Victims, which was surrounded in quietness to commemorate the deceased. I faced them in a room where we could hear the sound of running water, which many *hibakusha* were so desperate to drink before they died.

While I spoke with them, I showed them some photos, including the "boy with a red back" and another shot of my back taken a few years before. But as they listened to my talk, they didn't ask any questions, nor did they tell why they visited me. Gradually I became angry, and soon I found myself taking off my jacket and shirt to expose the scars on my back.

Some studies point out that the U.S wanted to test the uranium and plutonium-type bombs to show off their military muscle and take the advantage in the post-World War II diplomacy. I agree with this perspective. I knew it would be of no use to complain to his grandson about the results of Truman's experiment on the human body, but I really wanted them to know and feel our suffering from the bottom of their hearts.

Even though many decades have passed, I can never forgive the dropping of the atomic bombs. I wanted to live my youth like other young men did; I wanted to live a normal life. The U.S may never apologize to us for the atomic bombing. That's OK, but only if they actually carry out the abolition of nuclear weapons. That would be the best apology for us.

Daniel told me, "The most important thing is for us to remember the true damage caused by the atomic bomb. I want to do my best to do whatever I can." He confessed to me that he had a plan to publish a book in the U.S. The following year he visited Nagasaki again and listened to me and other *hibakusha* about our experiences.

I think it will gather a lot of attention if the grandson of Truman writes about his experience of meeting with the *hibakusha*. I hope that his book will send out an appeal to the world about the damage caused by the atomic bombs and the necessity to prevent the creation of new sufferers of nuclear weapons.

Inspired by encounters

In the spring of 2013, Nihon Hidankyo received a letter from the United States from a 16 year old high school student. This student, who aspired to work in politics, had learned of my experience as an A-bomb survivor in an American History class and was inspired. The letter said, "I promise to make efforts so that all the survivors' struggles will not be in vain."

Receiving these kinds of letters from abroad or having strangers visit us happens often.

One day in the late 1980s, a girl from Germany who was fresh out of high school visited us all by herself, despite the fact that she could hardly speak Japanese. Her name was Ulrike Dammers.

She told me that reading the novel which described half my life, "The Postman of Nagasaki," had made her determined to meet me by any means possible. She stayed with us for half a month, and we took her around Hiroshima and Tokyo. For some reason she treated me like a father, and said that she "wanted to immigrate to Japan." I had to persuade her by saying, "You have to return to your parents in Germany."

She was a good-hearted girl, yet her stubbornness made things difficult for us at times. When she didn't listen to us, my wife said to her, "If you don't listen, I'll cook potatoes for dinner!" Even though potatoes are a dietary staple in Germany, Ulrike couldn't stand them. My wife and I couldn't help but laugh when she calmed down straightaway saying, "No potatoes!" I heard that she engaged in peace movements for a while after returning to Germany.

Another unexpected encounter took place at the 2010 NPT Review Conference. A Japanese woman living in New York came to visit me at the hotel where I was staying. Her name was Ms. Tatebayashi Ai, an illustrator for a women's magazine. She told me she wanted to tell my story in a picture book.

I showed her my burnt back at the hotel and told her about my experience as an A-bomb survivor. Ms. Tatebayashi has visited me twice in Nagasaki since then, and listened intently as I told her of my journey over the years. The last time I met her, it appeared that her illustrations were nearly finished. She was hopeful as she told me that she wished for her work to be published in the United States. That made me happy.

People of various backgrounds from many countries have felt something through me and are taking action. I really feel that these encounters are fueling my activism.

For the love of my hometown

When I wake up every morning, I always bring some cooked rice as an offering to the Karasuiwa Shrine, located right down from my house. After placing the offering, I drum on the Shrine's large taiko. My neighbors have told me that the echo of the drums every morning around seven o'clock is like an alarm clock for them.

Ever since my grandmother took me in when I was just a year

old, I have lived on the hillsides of Mount Inasa in Nagasaki City. It's my home, and the shrine has always been a part of my life.

I took on the role of the shrine's guardian about 40 years ago, when a carpenter who had been responsible was no longer able due to his old age. He loved me as if I were his nephew, always calling out to me, "Sumi!" One day he brought me the keys to the shrine and asked me to give offerings in his place. I haven't missed a day since. When I travel overseas to share my story, my wife takes on the role. "You agreed to it too easily," she complains, but she still does the job; she doesn't forget to drum on the taiko either.

Every year in autumn, the Hiradogoya-kunchi Festival of the Karasuiwa Shrine takes place. Back in the day we used to celebrate the eve of the festival by spending the night at the shrine and having a pre-festival party. But not anymore. Both the number of participants and organizers of the festival have decreased over the years. Ever since Hiradogoya-machi was divided in two in 1965, I feel people's interest in the festival has diminished.

I think one of the reasons is the changes in the people living here. Hiradogoya-kunchi Festival is a festival to pray for the safety of sea voyages. In the old days many sailors lived in this town, so their families would always come to the festivals to pay their respects at the shrine. In 1989, the Nagasaki Fishery Port moved to the northwestern part of the city, and a lot of residents moved with it. The number of fishing boats have declined too. There are hardly any people from the olden days left.

But despite all that, the festival in the autumn of 2012 saw 200 participants. After the performance of Tai Chi and other dedicatory dances, the scattering of caramel candies commences. The individually wrapped caramels stay clean when they fall to the ground, and the children have a lot of fun picking them. It's been going on for more than 20 years now. In a square that looks down on the Nagasaki Port, officers from the Residents' Association scatter them from the top of a rock.

Although I am supposed to behave as a long-serving facilitator of this festival on behalf of the Shrine board and residents, I turn back into a kid on these occasions; I race to get the caramels alongside the children.

I believe such local events should be carried on by those who have lived here. We all wish for our children to grow healthy and strong, with respect and love for their home town, even once they become adults.

My inner child coming out at the caramel scattering.

Let Nagasaki be the last A-bombed site

In the spring of 2012, an association of second-generation atomic bomb sufferers was founded within the Nagasaki Hisaikyo where I serve as president. It had not been organized earlier because those children were too busy with their jobs or parenting, and they were also worried about being subject to prejudice.

The inauguration of this association shows that we are running short on time. The Nagasaki Hisaikyo was founded in 1956 with a membership of 30,000, but now after half a century, the number has dwindled to 10,000. Mr. Yamaguchi Senji, one of the founding organizers and my comrade passed away in July 2013.

The Second Generation Sufferers' Association is currently vigorously active, listening to their parents' recounting of A-bomb experiences and deepening exchanges with other second generation sufferers from Fukuoka, Kumamoto, and Kagoshima Prefectures in the Kyushu area. They are also following in our footsteps of seeking the elimination of nuclear weapons and improving and expanding official measures for A-bomb survivors. Nihon Hidankyo has also founded its Second Generation Sufferers' Committee and such succession efforts have been spreading throughout the country.

I myself have hopes for my daughter and son to carry on my work after they retire. I have not formally spoken to them about my experiences as a victim or our movement, nor have they asked me to.

Yet they have grown up emulating my life, seeing me suffer from my back burns and giving talks overseas, so I am sure they know what to do, even though I haven't asked them to.

I have four grandchildren. We have the hand and foot prints of the eldest daughter of my son Hideo on the decoration paper board that hangs on the wall in our house. Her birthday is August

9, 2004. By what twist of fate I do not know, she was born on the same day the atomic bomb was dropped on Nagasaki. Hideo must have known how I felt, seeing as he brought her handprints and footprints on a *shikishi* (decorative colored paper).

The A-bomb took the lives of several tens of thousands in an instant. Having my entire back burnt, I nearly perished then. I believe I was left to live with the pain and agony until the day I die, staying alive with the support from my family and kin, friends in the same circumstances as me, and all the people who pray for peace. Our desperate wish for the elimination of nuclear weapons is yet to be achieved. Having to entrust this responsibility to the generations of our children or grandchildren is regretful and frustrating. If only as a parting gift by a dying man, I have to at least set a course for the abolition of nuclear weapons.

What I have told you so far is the experience of just one victim. To cover all the damage caused by the A-bomb is not possible. But please, visit Nagasaki or Hiroshima and listen to a sufferer's story, even if just one. Then imagine as you listen, someone special to you turning into ashes or seeing yourself immersed in despair at the nuclear site. Engrave that sight unto your hearts and I hope that it will be reflected in your actions. Individual voices, however small they are, should turn into public opinion, influence politics, and change the world. I too will continue to speak out with all the strength of life left in me.

Let Nagasaki be the last atomic bombed site; let us be the last victims. Let the voice for the elimination of nuclear weapons spread all over the world.

The Atomic Bomb On My Back

I will continue to speak out for the elimination of nuclear weapons
with all the strength of life left in me.

Chronological Record of the Life of Taniguchi Sumiteru

Movement of Taniguchi and Hibakusha	World and domestic movement over nuclear weapons
1929 (Showa 4) Jan - Born in former Shiga Village, Kasuya-gun (current Higashi-ku, Fukuoka City) of Fukuoka Prefecture on January 26th.	
1930 (Showa 5) Mother dies from illness. Taken in by his grandmother in Nagasaki.	
	1938 (Showa 13) Apr - National General Mobilisation Act promulgated.
	1939 (Showa 14) WWII breaks out.
	1941 (Showa 16) Pacific War starts.
	1942 (Showa 17) US Manhattan Project starts.
1943 (Showa 18) Employed by Nagasaki Motohakata Post Office.	
1945 (Showa 20) Aug - A-bombed in Nagasaki City, 1.8km away from epicentre. Sep - Admitted to Shinkozen Temporary Relief Station Nov - Admitted to Omura Naval Hospital. Long hospital stay begins.	**1945** (Showa 20) Feb - US, UK and USSR leaders meet at Yalta Conference. Aug - Uranium atomic bomb dropped in Hiroshima (6th). Plutonium bomb dropped in Nagasaki (9th). Japan accepts the Potsdam Declaration. WWII ends (15th). Sep - GHQ orders a press code (press restraints).
1949 (Showa 24) Discharged from hospital in March; Reinstated to the Nagasaki Telegraph Office in April.	**1949** (Showa 24) Aug - USSR's first atomic bomb testing.
	1950 (Showa 25) Jun - Korean War begins.
1951 (Showa 26) Facial surgery of the jaw and left cheek, due to ulcer from bedsores.	**1951** (Showa 26) Sep - San Francisco peace treaty and Japan-US Security Treaty signed.
	1952 (Showa 27) Oct - UK's first atomic bomb testing. Nov - US' first hydrogen bomb testing.
1953 (Showa 28) Nagasaki Atomic Bomb Maidens Association founded.	**1953** (Showa 28) Aug - USSR's first hydrogen bomb testing.
1954 (Showa 29) May - Suginami Association for the Signature Campaign against Hydrogen Bombs formed.	**1954** (Showa 29) Mar - Lucky Dragon No.5 (Daigo Fukuryu Maru), tuna fishing boat, exposed to radiation from US hydrogen bomb testing at Bikini Atoll.

The Atomic Bomb On My Back

Movement of Taniguchi and Hibakusha	World and domestic movement over nuclear weapons
1955 (Showa 30) Oct - Nagasaki Atomic Bomb Youth Association starts.	**1955** (Showa 30) Aug - First World Conference against Atomic and Hydrogen Bombs held in Hiroshima. Sep - Japan Council against Atomic and Hydrogen Bombs (Gensuikyo) initiated
1956 (Showa 31) Mar - Marries Eiko. May - Nagasaki Atomic Bomb Maidens Association and Nagasaki Atomic Bomb Youth Association merge to form Nagasaki Atomic Bomb Youth and Maidens Association. Jun - Nagasaki Atomic Bomb Survivors Council created. Aug - Japan Confederation of A-and H-Bomb Sufferers Organizations (Nihon Hidankyo) founded on the 2nd day of the World Conference against A and H Bombs.	**1956** (Showa 31) Aug - Second World Conference against A & H Bombs held in Nagasaki.
1957 (Showa 32) Jul - Daughter Sumie is born.	**1957** (Showa 32) Apr - Atomic Bomb Sufferers' Medical Care Act enforced.
1958 (Showa 33) May - The Japanese Red Cross Nagasaki Atomic Bomb Hospital opens.	
1959 (Showa 34) Sep - Son Hideo is born	
1960 (Showa 35) First surgery to remove a foreign body protruding from beneath the cicatrix on his back.	**1960** (Showa 35) Jan - Revised Japan-US Security Treaty signed. Campaign against this treaty launched.
1961 (Showa 36) Travels to East Germany for medical treatment.	**1961** (Showa 36) National Council for Peace and against Nuclear Weapons (Kakkin- Kaigi) founded.
	1962 (Showa 37) Anti-nuclear movement divided over USSR nuclear testing.
	1963 (Showa 38) Aug - US, UK and USSR sign Partial Test Ban Treaty. World Conference against A & H Bombs divides over the evaluation of this treaty.
	1965 (Showa 40) Feb - Japan Congress against Atomic and Hydrogen Bombs (Gensuikin) created.
1966 (Showa 41) Nihon Hidankyo publishes a pamphlet "Characteristics of the A-Bomb Damage and Demand for a Hibakusha Aid Law" (Tsuru Pamphlet).	

Chronological Record of the Life of Taniguchi Sumiteru

Movement of Taniguchi and Hibakusha	World and domestic movement over nuclear weapons
	1968 (Showa 43) Sep - Law Concerning Special Measures for the Atomic Bomb Exposed enforced.
1970 (Showa 45) Jun - Photograph of Taniguchi's crimson burnt back published in Asahi Shimbun, bringing him to the center stage of Hibakusha movement.	
	1972 (Showa 47) May - US and USSR sign SALT I (Strategic Arms Limitation Talks). Okinawa returned to homeland Japan.
1974 (Showa 49) Aug - Participates in the Nagasaki peace memorial ceremony for the first time and reads "A Pledge for Peace."	
1975 (Showa 50) Appeals for enactment of Hibakusha Aid Law in the House of Representative's Budget Committee.	**1975** (Showa 50) Gensuikyo and Nihon Hidankyo travel to New York to request the UN to conclude an international agreement for a total ban on nuclear weapons.
1977 (Showa 52) Protests against the acceptance of atomic powered ship "Mutsu" at Sasebo Port.	**1977** (Showa 52) Aug - World Conference against A & H Bombs is held by united efforts in Hiroshima after 14 years of division
1978 (Showa 53) Travels to Geneva and Romania together with Watanabe Chieko to take part in NGO International Conference on Disarmament.	**1978** (Showa 53) First UN Special Session on Disarmament (SSD-I)
	1979 (Showa 54) Jun - US and USSR sign SALT II.
1980 (Showa 55) Jul - Nagasaki Citizens Association against Nuclear Tests is created and Taniguchi assumes the post of its representative.	**1980** (Showa 55) Dec - Ministry of Welfare's advisory body Council on Basic Problems of the Atomic Bombing and Measures for the Survivors (Kihonkon) concludes that the A-bomb damage must be endured.
1982 (Showa 57) Jun - Participates in the 1-million people rally and march in New York; visits local cities in the US on a speaking tour.	**1982** (Showa 57) Jun - 2nd UN Special Session for Disarmament (SDD-II).
1984 (Showa 59) Peter Townsend, former UK Royal Air Force Group Captain publishes "The Postman of Nagasaki."	

The Atomic Bomb On My Back

Movement of Taniguchi and Hibakusha	World and domestic movement over nuclear weapons
1986 (Showa 61) Retires from Nagasaki Telegraph Office before mandatory retirement age. Participates in Hidankyo's speaking tour in the US.	**1986** (Showa 61) **Apr** - Chernobyl nuclear power plant accident in the Republic of Ukraine, USSR. **Aug** - World Conference against A & H Bombs splits again.
	1987 (Showa 62) **Dec** - US and USSR sign a treaty on the total elimination of Intermediate Range Nuclear Forces.
	1988 (Showa 63) 3rd UN Special Session for Disarmament (SSD-III).
1989 (Heisei 1) Protests against port call of USS Rodney M. Davis to Nagasaki Port.	**1989** (Heisei 1) Cold War ends.
	1991 (Heisei 3) **Jul** - US and USSR sign Strategic Arms Reduction Treaty (START I).
	1993 (Heisei 5) **Jan** - US and Russia sign START II.
	1994 (Heisei 6) **Dec** - Hibakusha Relief Law enacted.
	1995 (Heisei 7) 50th Anniversary of Atomic Bombings.
	1996 (Heisei 8) **Jul** - International Court of Justice issues an Advisory Opinion saying that nuclear weapons would generally be contrary to International Law.
2000 (Heisei 12) **Jul** - Nagasaki A-bomb survivor Matsuya Hideko's lawsuit triumphs in the Supreme Court gaining official recognition of A-bomb-induced illness.	**2000** (Heisei 12) **May** - NPT Review Conference agrees on "An unequivocal undertaking by the nuclear weapon States to accomplish the total elimination of their nuclear arsenals leading to nuclear disarmament."
	2001 (Heisei 13) Terrorist attacks of Sept. 11, 2001 in USA.
2003 (Heisei 15) Collective lawsuits for the recognition of A-bomb related illnesses filed.	
2004 (Heisei 16) Participates in Preparatory Committee of the NPT Review Conference and requested ambassadors of States parties to eliminate nuclear weapons.	**2004** (Heisei 16) 3rd Preparatory Committee for the 2005 NPT Review Conference held in the US.

Chronological Record of the Life of Taniguchi Sumiteru

Movement of Taniguchi and Hibakusha	World and domestic movement over nuclear weapons
2005 (Heisei 17) First Atomic Bomb exhibition at UN held during the NPT Review Conference.	2005 (Heisei 17) May - NPT Review Conference.
2006 (Heisei 18) Assumes President of Nagasaki A-Bomb Survivors Council.	
2008 (Heisei 20) Japanese government relaxes criteria for recognising A-bomb related illness in 2008-09, after having consecutively lost in the Collective lawsuits filed by the Hibakusha.	
2009 (Heisei 21) May - Nobel Peace Prize laureates issue the "Hiroshima-Nagasaki Declaration."	2009 (Heisei 21) Apr - Prague speech of US President Obama.
2010 (Heisei 22) May - Taniguchi Assumes the position of Co-Chairperson of Nihon Hidankyo. Makes a speech at the NPT Review Conference.	2010 (Heisei 22) May - NPT Review Conference.
	2011 (Heisei 23) Mar - The Great East Japan Earthquake and Fukushima Daiichi Nuclear Power Plant accident (11th).
2012 (Heisei 24) Aug - Taniguchi meets with Clifton Truman Daniel, grandson of President Truman who ordered the bombing of Hiroshima and Nagasaki. Tells him of his Atomic bomb experience.	2012 (Heisei 24) May - Switzerland and 15 other countries in the PrepCom of the NPT Review Conference issue a joint statement urging all States to "intensify their efforts to outlaw nuclear weapons."
2013 (Heisei 25) Jul - Senji Yamaguchi passes away.	2013 (Heisei 25) Dec - Japanese government announces new criteria for recognition of A- bomb related illnesses, which is criticized by the Hibakusha.

AFTERWORD

I FIRST HEARD MR. TANIGUCHI'S LIFE story in October 2011, in a room of Nagasaki Council of Atomic Bomb Survivors (Nagasaki Hisaikyo), an organization for which he served as President.

Around that time, I was preparing for a series of articles about the co-produced Japanese-French film, "Typhon sur Nagasaki (Printemps a Nagasaki)," shot in Nagasaki in 1956, which was to be screened in the city after many years. Thanks to the big film stars from both countries, Nagasaki City was filled with excitement at the time of the filming, and the basic infrastructure of the city was reconstructed at a rapid rate in time for shooting, which helped Nagasaki to become a tourist city. It is said that the streetscape of Nagasaki captured in the film and shown in color in Japan and internationally changed the image of the A-bombed city, which had once been described as a "barren field."

Thinking that this film, which symbolized the "recovery from the A-bomb damage" should have given some inspiration to the *hibakusha*, I visited Mr. Taniguchi and asked him about the film. His answer was completely different from what I had expected. Not only did he have never seen the film, he also described bitterly how the streetscape of Nagasaki became cleaner and

Afterword

cleaner around that time, saying, "To me it seemed as if they were trying to get rid of the abhorrent scars of the A-bombing as quickly as possible."

As told in this book, 12 years after the end of the war, no public relief measures for the *hibakusha* had been taken, and the *hibakusha* were exposed to unprovoked discrimination in employment and marriage. It was only the year following the release of the film that the survivors lifted themselves up and achieved the enactment of the Act for Atomic Bomb Sufferers' Medical Care. I remember the shook I felt at my own ignorance about the A-bomb survivors struggle to live and work to achieve official relief measures, while ordinary citizens were only passionate about the film. This sentiment seemed to be in the background of my undertaking of the serial interviews "*Genbaku wo seotte* (Having the A-Bomb on My Back)" of Mr. Taniguchi.

In this book, I intended to describe Mr. Taniguchi just as he is, a person whose life was derailed by the atomic bombing and who has struggled to survive to this day. After sustaining permanent scars, due to the photograph of his reddened back becoming public, he has come to assume the role as a "representative face of the *hibakusha*," and with some hesitation has gradually emerged at the frontline of the movement. It is the author's hope that through this book, not only Mr. Taniguchi's anger, sadness, or pain, but also his personality – stubborn but sometimes mischievous – will be conveyed to readers.

Mr. Taniguchi is a person with a strong sense of responsibility. As he says, this disposition was perhaps formed over a long period of enduring enormous suffering. I imagine that it was out of his sense of responsibility to pass on the memories of the *hibakusha* to future generations that he kindly responded to my interviews, which lasted almost a year, despite his ill health. I cannot express my appreciation and respect enough to Mr. Taniguchi. Also, it goes without saying that this book would not have been possible without the support and advice of so many people.

We will soon commemorate the 70th anniversary of the end of the Second World War. It has long been warned that the experiences of the *hibakusha* would get lost in oblivion. True, the time left for us to listen directly to the living testimonies of the *hibakusha* is indeed very limited. I hope that people will visit Nagasaki or Hiroshima in person and listen to the stories of as many *hibakusha* as possible. I myself will continue to cover and write about the *hibakusha*.

It is my sincere hope that this book will help to convey the ardent aspiration for peace of the *hibakusha*, who have dedicated their lives to the abolition of nuclear weapons and to the betterment of relief measures for victims of the atomic bombings.

Summer 2014
Hisashi Tomokuni